THE
FOUNTAINHEAD

Ayn Rand

TECHNICAL DIRECTOR Maxwell Krohn
EDITORIAL DIRECTOR Justin Kestler
MANAGING EDITOR Ben Florman

SERIES EDITORS Boomie Aglietti, Justin Kestler
PRODUCTION Christian Lorentzen

WRITERS Julio Machado, Bulbul Tiwari
EDITORS Thomas Connors, Emma Chastain

This edition published by Spark Publishing

Spark Publishing
A Division of SparkNotes LLC
120 Fifth Avenue, 8th Floor
New York, NY 10011

02 03 04 05 SN 9 8 7 6 5 4 3 2 1

Please send all comments and questions or report errors to
feedback@sparknotes.com.

Library of Congress information available upon request

Printed and bound in the United States

RRD-C

ISBN 1-58663-515-8

INTRODUCTION: STOPPING TO BUY SPARKNOTES ON A SNOWY EVENING

Whose words these are you *think* you know.
Your paper's due tomorrow, though;
We're glad to see you stopping here
To get some help before you go.

Lost your course? You'll find it here.
Face tests and essays without fear.
Between the words, good grades at stake:
Get great results throughout the year.

Once school bells caused your heart to quake
As teachers circled each mistake.
Use SparkNotes and no longer weep,
Ace every single test you take.

Yes, books are lovely, dark, and deep,
But only what you grasp you keep,
With hours to go before you sleep,
With hours to go before you sleep.

Contents

NOTE: This SparkNote refers to the Bobbs-Merrill Company, Inc., 1968 edition of *The Fountainhead*.

CONTEXT

AYN RAND WAS BORN to an affluent upper-middle-class family on February 2, 1905, in St. Petersburg, Russia. Rand formulated many of her strongly held beliefs early in life. Although her family was nominally Jewish, Rand thought of religion as a form of mysticism and became a committed atheist at the age of fourteen. She was passionately interested in politics, particularly after the beginning of the Russian Revolution in 1917. When the Bolshevik Party came to power at the end of 1917, it nationalized Rand's father's business and diminished the family's fortunes considerably. Rand opposed the Bolsheviks' ideals, which included communism, socialism, and collectivization.

Rand graduated from the University of Petrograd with highest honors in philosophy and history. In 1925, Rand obtained a temporary visa to visit relatives in Chicago. She left Russia with no intention of returning. She moved to Hollywood to pursue a career as a screenwriter and took a job as an extra on the set of *King of Kings,* a film directed by the legendary Cecil B. DeMille. In California, Rand met Frank O'Connor, whom she married in 1929.

Over the next several years, Rand moved from job to job in Hollywood. In 1932, she sold her first screenplay, *Red Pawn,* to Universal Studios. That same year, Rand's first stage play, *Night of January 16th,* was produced in Hollywood and then on Broadway. She completed her first novel, *We the Living,* in 1933, but all of the publishers she approached rejected the manuscript until 1936, when Macmillan published the novel in the United States. The novel was based on Rand's life in Russia and drew strong criticism from leftist members of the American intelligentsia. Rand began work on *The Fountainhead* in 1938. Again she had trouble finding a publisher, but eventually Bobbs-Merrill accepted the novel in 1941. Over the next two years, *The Fountainhead*'s reputation grew by word of mouth and the novel became a bestseller when it came out in 1943.

In 1957, Rand published *Atlas Shrugged*. By this time her work had inspired a devoted following. Rand made numerous public appearances to lecture and explain the ideas behind her work. Rand disliked being associated with either the conservative or libertarian political movements in the United States. She felt her ideas were distinct and started her own movement, called Objectivism, which promoted her conception of rational self-interest and denounced altruism. *The Fountainhead* embodies Rand's Objectivist philosophy, suggesting that egoism is an absolute moral good and therefore any person, institution, or system that blocks an individual's freedom and talent is evil. *The Fountainhead* is an Objectivist parable. Each character in the novel represents a different level on the spectrum of good and evil. Like the authors of other satirical and allegorical works, Rand does not create complex, three-dimensional characters, but designs personalities to prove a point.

During the 1950s and 1960s, Rand promoted her ideas with the help of two young protégés, Nathaniel and Barbara Branden. Rand's affair with Nathaniel Branden put an end to her alliance with the young couple. Rand died in her apartment in New York City on March 6, 1982. At the time of Rand's death, more than twenty million copies of her books had been sold. Rand's work continues to draw heated reactions from critics. She has been called a fascist, and some call her admirers devotees and worshippers, and even go so far as to call Objectivism a cult. Nonetheless, the Ayn Rand Institute and the Objectivist Center continue their work in America, and Rand's novels still attract a global following.

Plot Overview

HOWARD ROARK, A BRILLIANT YOUNG ARCHITECT, is expelled from his architecture school for refusing to follow the school's outdated traditions. He goes to New York to work for Henry Cameron, a disgraced architect whom Roark admires. Roark's schoolmate, Peter Keating, moves to New York and goes to work for the prestigious architectural firm Francon & Heyer, run by the famous Guy Francon. Roark and Cameron create beautiful work, but their projects rarely receive recognition, whereas Keating's ability to flatter and please brings him almost instant success. In just a few years, he becomes a partner at the firm after he causes Francon's previous partner to have a stroke. Henry Cameron retires, financially ruined, and Roark opens his own small office. His unwillingness to compromise his designs in order to satisfy clients eventually forces him to close down the office and take a job at a granite quarry in Connecticut.

In Connecticut, Roark feels an immediate, passionate attraction to Dominique Francon, Guy Francon's temperamental and beautiful daughter. Society disgusts Dominique, and she has retreated to her family's estate to escape the mediocre architecture she sees all around her. One night, Roark enters the house and rapes her. Dominique discovers that this is what she had needed, but when she looks for Roark, he has left the quarry to design a building for a prominent New York businessman. Dominique returns to New York and discovers Roark's identity. She realizes that he designed a building she admires. Dominique and Roark begin to meet in secret, but in public she tries to sabotage his career and destroy him. Ellsworth Toohey, an architectural critic and socialist, slowly prepares to rise to power. He seeks to prevent men from excelling by teaching that talent and ability are of no great consequence, and that the greatest virtue is humility. Toohey sees Roark as a great threat and tries to destroy him. Toohey convinces a weak-minded businessman named Hopton Stoddard to hire Roark as the designer for a temple dedicated to the human spirit, then persuades the businessman to sue Roark once the building is completed. At Roark's trial, every prominent architect in New York testifies that Roark's style is unorthodox and illegitimate, but Dominique declares that the world does not deserve the gift Roark has given it. Stoddard wins the case and Roark loses his business again. To punish herself for desiring Roark, Dominique marries Peter Keating.

Enter Gail Wynand, a brilliant publisher, who has lost his early idealism and made his fortune by printing newspapers that say exactly what the public wants to hear. Wynand meets Dominique and falls in love with her, so he buys her from Keating by offering him money and a prestigious contract in exchange for his wife. Dominique agrees to marry Wynand because she thinks he is an even worse person than Keating, but to her surprise, Wynand is a man of principle. Wynand and Roark meet and become fast friends, but Wynand does not know the truth about Roark's relationship with Dominique. Meanwhile Keating, who has fallen from grace, asks Roark for help with the Cortlandt Homes, a public housing project. The idea of economical housing intrigues Roark. He agrees to design the project and let Keating take the credit on the condition that no one makes a single alteration to his plan.

When Roark returns from a summer-long yacht trip with Wynand, he finds that, despite the agreement, the Cortlandt Homes project has been changed. Roark asks Dominique to distract the night watchman one night and then dynamites the building. When the police arrive, he submits without resistance. The entire country condemns Roark, but Wynand finally finds the courage to follow his convictions and orders his newspapers to defend him. The *Banner*'s circulation drops and the workers go on strike, but Wynand keeps printing with Dominique's help. Eventually, Wynand gives in and denounces Roark. At the trial, Roark seems doomed, but he rouses the courtroom with a statement about the value of selfishness and the need to remain true to oneself. Roark describes the triumphant role of creators and the price they pay at the hands of corrupt societies. The jury finds him not guilty. Roark marries Dominique. Wynand asks Roark to design one last building, a skyscraper that will testify to the supremacy of man.

CHARACTER LIST

*Howard Roark*The novel's hero, a brilliant architect of absolute
    integrity. Roark has friends and colleagues, but relies
    on himself alone. He is tall, gaunt, and angular, with
    gray eyes and distinctive orange hair. Born to a poor
    family, Roark supports himself throughout high school
    and college by working odd jobs on construction sites.
    He brings the same fiery intensity to whatever job he
    does, whether it is manual labor or architecture. He
    loves the beautiful Dominique Francon with violent
    passion. He is the novel's idealization of man, bringing
    innovative and joyful buildings to the rest of the world.

*Ellsworth Toohey*The villain of the novel, and Roark's
    antithesis—a man with a lust for power but no talent.
    Since his boyhood, Toohey has despised the
    achievements of others, and he dedicates himself to
    squelching other people's talents and ambitions. He is a
    small and fragile-looking man, but his persuasive voice
    and knack for manipulation make him a formidable
    opponent. He encourages selflessness and altruism to
    coax others into submission. His philosophy is a blend
    of religion, Fascism and Socialism, and he at times
    resembles the Russian dictator Joseph Stalin.

*Dominique Francon*Daughter of the prestigious architect Guy
    Francon, her fragile appearance, pale gold hair, and
    gray eyes belie her capability and bluntness.
    Dispassionate, cynical, and cold, Dominique nurses a
    masochistic streak. Although she loves Roark and his
    beliefs, she initially tries to destroy him before the rest
    of the world can. Eventually, to punish herself for her
    behavior, she marries Peter Keating and then Gail
    Wynand.

Gail Wynand A ruthless media tycoon who sells his integrity for power. Wynand comes from New York's slums and is an entirely self-taught, self-made man. He had sought power so he could rule the incompetent and corrupt, but in acquiring wealth he becomes like them. His faith in humanity is restored when he meets Roark, who is incorruptible, and he becomes Roark's great ally and friend before finally betraying him.

Peter Keating A classmate of Roark's who lives only for fame and the approval of others. Keating is good-looking and commercially successful, but he steals his only original ideas from Roark. In order to rise to the top, Keating flatters, lies, steals, kills, and even trades his wife, Dominique, for the opportunity to work on a promising project. His fall is even more rapid than his rise. He realizes the error of his ways too late and lives the rest of his life in frightened misery.

Henry Cameron Roark's mentor, an intractable and aggressive architect who is in the twilight of his career at the onset of the novel. Like Roark, Cameron suffers greatly at the hands of the world because he loves his buildings, but he does not have Roark's strength and lives a frustrated and anguished life. Ruined physically and financially, Cameron dies still fighting the world.

Catherine Halsey Toohey's niece and Keating's on-again, off-again fiancée. Halsey is not beautiful, but her innocence and sincerity provide Keating with a refuge from himself. Although Keating loves Katie, he abandons her, and her uncle Toohey slowly destroys her spirit.

Guy Francon Dominique's father and Keating's employer and business partner. Francon rises to fame nearly as swiftly as Keating, but he has no real talent of his own. Nonetheless, Francon is a fundamentally honest and decent man, and eventually he finds salvation through his love for his spirited daughter.

Stephen Mallory A gifted but disillusioned sculptor who feels alone and misunderstood until Roark rescues him from his drunken doldrums. Mallory's statues portray a heroic vision of man, but the world rejects his work. Mallory tries to kill Toohey, whom the artist blames for the failings of the world. Eventually he regains his self-confidence through his work on Roark's buildings.

Alvah Scarret Wynand's editor-in-chief. Scarret clings to Wynand out of habit and inertia. He believes every article and column printed in the *Banner*. Because Scarret's beliefs reflect those of the masses, Wynand uses him to measure public opinion.

Mrs. Keating Keating's forceful and manipulative mother. Mrs. Keating's preoccupation with money and success prompt Keating to make all the wrong choices. Mrs. Keating devoutly believes that financial success is the surest indicator of a person's quality.

Mike A tough, phenomenally ugly electrician who admires talent in any form. He instantly recognizes Roark's ability and becomes a staple on the construction sites of the buildings Roark designs.

The Dean The Dean of the architecture school, a staunch traditionalist who frowns on any deviation from the architectural canon. The Dean believes everything worthy has already been designed and views Roark as dangerous.

John Erik Snyte A supposedly progressive architect who is in fact the ultimate plagiarizer. He has a group of five designers who make their own version of each design and then puts together all of the five designs to create the final sketch.

ANALYSIS OF MAJOR CHARACTERS

HOWARD ROARK

Howard Roark is the undisputed hero of *The Fountainhead,* and his story drives the novel. His name contains the words "hard" and "roar," both of which accurately describe his tough, determined character. Roark's buildings suggest his personality, for like Roark they are innovative and austere. Roark never compromises or deviates from his principles. Rand holds him up as everything that man can and should be. Consequently, Roark does not develop over the course of the novel—the ideal man does not need to change. Although Rand despised religion, she often describes Roark as if he is a religious figure. Roark does not preach, and he never actively seeks converts, but he inspires absolute devotion and rapture in his followers. Cameron, Mallory, Dominique, and Wynand change their entire belief systems after meeting him. Dominique in particular exhibits a religious passion for Roark, racked by ecstasy and guilt as if inspired by a messiah. Like all Christ figures in literature, Roark's enemies persecute him. Despite the hatred of the world, Roark lives life as Rand thinks it should be lived.

ELLSWORTH TOOHEY

In direct contrast to Roark, Ellsworth Monkton Toohey embodies everything evil about mankind. He is irredeemably corrupt and evil. Whereas Roark never tries to win friends or influence people, Toohey's power lies entirely in his ability to control weaker minds and souls. Toohey's evil is as ingrained as Roark's goodness—Toohey learns the practice of manipulation as a child, and turns it into an art by the time he graduates from college. By making people feel small and guilty, Toohey shakes their faith in their own abilities and then assumes control of their lives. Toohey preaches selflessness and ignorance of the ego to force people to act with humble mediocrity. Toohey has no talents of his own, so he makes himself excellent by grinding down his followers. His tactics frequently evoke those of

Joseph Stalin, the former Russian revolutionary who emerged as Russia's dictator.

DOMINIQUE FRANCON

Dominique's beauty and strength of spirit make her a perverse, unusual woman and the perfect complement to Howard Roark. At the beginning of the novel, she is convinced of the world's rottenness and believes that greatness has no chance of survival. She surrounds herself with the things she despises to avoid watching the world destroy the things she loves. Dominique instantly recognizes Roark's greatness, but she does not initially believe that he can survive in a selfless and irrational society. The thought that a man like Roark needs society in order to build pains Dominique, and she tries to destroy him before the rest of the world can. Yet Dominique wants to fail in her bid to destroy Roark, because if she fails it means absolute good and genius can survive even in an evil world.

GAIL WYNAND

The charismatic, capable, and aristocratic Wynand straddles the line between mainstream society and Roark's world, and this division makes him the novel's tragic figure. Like Roark, Wynand has extraordinary capabilities and energy, but unlike Roark he lets the world corrupt him. When we first meet Wynand, he is entirely a man of the outside world, exclusively involved with society and its interests. His youthful idealism has been crushed by the world's cynicism. Wynand makes his living with newspapers that report on the vulgar and the common. This involvement with the world leaves Wynand misanthropic, bored, and suicidal. Wynand's worldview changes when he meets Dominique and Roark, who ignite the passion and integrity lingering within Wynand. During Roark's trial Wynand fights the world again and tries to turn his life around. He eventually feels that he cannot escape the ugliness he has created. Tragically, Wynand compromises at the last minute and loses his last chance at salvation.

PETER KEATING

Rand has little sympathy for the rise and fall of Peter Keating. Keating starts off as a young and attractive architecture student, and although he is clearly Roark's inferior, their lives and careers advance in parallel fashion. By the novel's end, however, Keating is a weak and alcoholic nobody, the exact fate once reserved for talented men like Henry Cameron. Whereas Cameron suffers because of others, however, Keating is a victim of his own mistakes. Unlike Wynand, who suffers for turning his back on his own potential, Keating is born mediocre and weak and never had a chance at greatness. Instead, Keating suffers for denying his own mediocrity and for thinking himself too good for a modest but happy life. In *The Fountainhead*, character determines fate, and the moment Keating becomes dishonest as well as weak, he dooms himself to unhappiness.

CHARACTER ANALYSIS

THEMES, MOTIFS & SYMBOLS

THEMES

Themes are the fundamental and often universal ideas explored in a literary work.

THE PRIMACY OF THE INDIVIDUAL

Howard Roark is the novel's embodiment of the perfect man. Rand wants us to admire his talent and courage, and his struggle to resist society's sway and remain true to himself. *The Fountainhead* revolves around Roark's struggle to retain his individuality in the face of forces bent on bringing him to heel. At his second trial, Roark argues that individuals, not societies, propel history. He says that individual creators are *the fountainhead* of civilization. Roark's speech is passionate and lyrical, and the audience receives it with awed silence. The struggle for individuality is not confined to Roark. Every one of the novel's sympathetic characters struggles to act independently from society, and the desire to assert one's self becomes the single greatest virtue a character can possess. The novel ends triumphantly not because Roark defeats or converts his enemies, but because he has won the right to act according to his own principles. The thesis at the heart of *The Fountainhead* is that society has a herd mentality, and individuals must act selfishly in order to be free.

THE IMPORTANCE OF REASON

The Fountainhead disapproves of sentimentalism, and argues that everything worth thinking or feeling should be the product of reason and logic, not emotion. Whenever Roark, Dominique, or Wynand expound on the supremacy of the individual, they justify their positions with logical arguments rather than with emotional appeals. The novel respects logic and reason so much that everything it applauds is scientific, factual, and pure. The novel's mathematicians, engineers, builders, and businessmen are inevitably more intelligent than its sentimental writers and journalists. Roark bases all of his designs on the simplest geometrical shapes, such as triangles or squares. Rand condemns sentimentality and compassion as the enemies of reason because they confuse the mind and compromise individualism. The arch-villain Toohey controls the weak by advocating such values as selflessness. Collectivism, altruism, and mysticism are depicted as illogical beliefs that manipulate the heart rather than engage the mind. In order to justify the novel's tough attitude, Rand argues that even the best intentions lead to imprisonment, while cold, unflinching reason sets man free.

THE COLD FEROCITY OF LOVE

In *The Fountainhead*, love, like integrity and invention, is a principle worth fighting for and defending. The protagonists constantly hone and improve their relationships. Even Roark and Dominique forego some of their fierce devotion to independence and eventually allow themselves to surrender to one another. The emotion of love might seem to contradict the novel's devotion to reason, but the characters demand relationships so perfect that they come to seem logical and mathematical. Roark stands by while Dominique marries first Keating and then Wynand as if watching her enact an algebraic equation. He calculates that she will emerge from the marriages more suited to him, so he bears the pain of losing her to other men. Even in their passionate encounters, Roark and Dominique refuse to yield to emotion. Instead, they make love with a violent and calculating fury in scenes that Rand writes in prose more technical than romantic. The novel extols the virtues of science and logic and argues personal relationships can exist within these virtues. As long as relationships help people maximize their potential, then the novel sees love as a version of logic, and therefore approves of it.

MOTIFS

Motifs are recurring structures, contrasts, or literary devices that can help to develop and inform the text's major themes.

TECHNICAL PROGRESS

In *The Fountainhead*, technical progress indicates the forward movement of society. The novel measures the progress of mankind by the number of buildings and scientific innovations it produces, rather than by its art and philosophy. All of the most crucial industrial developments come from the minds of individuals and entrepreneurs rather than from the masses. Therefore, the period of greatest industrial development also marks the period of greatest individualism. Rand's adoring treatment of the New York skyline signals her glorification of industry and technology. Wynand, Dominique, and Roark all gaze admiringly at the skyline, which serves as a reminder of their ambitions and goals. Beautiful, inspired skyscrapers represent human conquest over nature and symbolize modernity. In contrast to this glorification of architecture, the novel scoffs at other forms of art. Every time a new play or work of literature crops up in the narrative, the work in question is made to appear ridiculous and self-indulgent.

JOURNALISM

The novel holds up architecture as the ideal art form, and journalism as all that is banal and corrupt. The villainous Toohey works his ill will as a sneaky, manipulative journalist, and Wynand builds his empire on a chain of exploitative and sensationalist papers that cater to the most depraved emotions of the masses. Rand constantly suggests the impossibility of reasoned, intelligent journalism. The one time Wynand tries to use his paper for good, he fails. According to Rand, newspapers are fundamentally weak because they have to cater to the public. The idiocy of the public becomes clear when Wynand holds a contest. He tests the public by trying to raise money simultaneously for a brilliant scientist and for the pregnant girlfriend of a convicted murderer. When the public overwhelmingly supports the girl, it suggests that the public is incapable of the rationality necessary to accomplish great things. Rand suggests that any medium that relies on the public is doomed to mediocrity.

LABOR

The novel exhibits mixed views on manual labor, regarding it as both one of the few authentic occupations and as a den of collectivist activity. Roark works at many construction sites, which allows him to preserve his integrity by earning wages when he cannot find clients. Roark has good friends who work as laborers, such as Mike the electrician. The novel presents physical labor as a pure, productive activity and thus something admirable. On the other hand, labor breeds unions, groups that the novel violently condemns. Nefarious Toohey makes his first appearance in the novel when he addresses a crowd of discontented laborers and easily manipulates their cooperative spirit to make them his spiritual captives. Rand

MOTIFS

was a virulent anti-communist and saw socialism, which grew out of the labor movement, as the greatest threat to the United States. The novel admires laborers and workmen as individuals, but it fears and mistrusts them as a group.

SYMBOLS

> *Symbols are objects, characters, figures, or colors used to represent abstract ideas or concepts.*

GRANITE

Rand associates granite with Roark's character. Granite symbolizes his external and internal features. Like the rock, Roark's face, body, and mind are hard, rare, unchanging, and beautiful. Roark, however, is even stronger than the rock that symbolizes him. In a number of scenes, we see Roark breaking granite or using it for his designs. When Dominique first sees Roark at a granite quarry she wishes the drilling would hurt and destroy Roark, but by the end of the novel, Roark's ability to shape the granite according to his desires pleases her. The novel believes in the absolute supremacy of man, and consequently it rejoices when man triumphs over nature.

ICE

Ice symbolizes Dominique. Rand describes Dominique's body as fragile and angular. The clothes that Dominique wears either glitter like ice, shine like glass, or are the color of water. Wynand gives Dominique a diamond necklace made to look like loose pieces of ice scattered on her cool skin. Ice also reflects her personality at the beginning of the novel—blank and frigid. Once Roark warms Dominique's spirit, the associations between her and ice grow infrequent and eventually disappear.

THE BANNER

In *The Fountainhead*, the *Banner* symbolizes the worst elements of society and mass culture. The *Banner* reflects and feeds the public's poor taste. In *The Fountainhead* only individuals are noble, so anything designed for a group is necessarily ugly, crude, and ignorant. Wynand realizes this fact at the very end of the novel when he tries to make the *Banner* into an honorable machine and finally sees that the newspaper cannot elevate public opinion to something noble.

Summary & Analysis

Part I: Chapters 1–5

Summary: Chapter 1

Howard Roark, a stern-faced young man, stands naked at the edge of a granite cliff. The year is 1922 and Roark has just been expelled from architecture school at the Stanton Institute of Technology. Although Roark excels in engineering and mathematics, he is an individualist whose modern designs run contrary to everything his school teaches. After serenely contemplating his future, Roark returns to his room in a local boardinghouse to work on his drawings. His designs seem severe and simple, but the structures are actually complex. Roark forgets that he has a meeting with the Dean of the college until his landlady, Mrs. Keating, whose son Peter is also a student at the architecture school, reminds him. Roark goes to see the Dean.

The Dean says that Roark was expelled for turning in overly modern designs. The Dean assures Roark that he may be able to return to the school once he has matured. Roark refuses the offer. The Dean is offended and informs Roark that he will never become a real architect. Roark leaves the Dean's office and thinks about how he does not understand men like the Dean.

Summary: Chapter 2

At the Stanton commencement ceremonies, Peter Keating sits reflecting on his own greatness. After the ceremony, Guy Francon, a prominent architect who has given the commencement speech, offers Keating a position in his firm. Keating does not know whether to accept the position or take a prestigious scholarship. When Keating returns home, he asks for Roark's opinion. Roark says that Peter should make his decisions without assistance. Peter's mother manipulates her son into taking Francon's offer. Roark agrees that the job will mean more actual building, and Keating is elated by his prospects.

Summary: Chapter 3

In New York, Keating begins working for Francon & Heyer, Francon's firm. He excels at office politics. Keating soon discovers that the brains behind the firm actually belong to a man named Claude Stengel, who acts as the chief draftsman and architect. Keating befriends Francon. Roark finds work with the architect Henry Cameron, a once-popular architect who has fallen from grace. Like Roark, Cameron loves his buildings more than his clients. Roark and Cameron work hard and talk little in their run-down and failing office.

SUMMARY: CHAPTER 4

Two years pass, and Keating scrambles further up the ladder at Francon & Heyer. He gets his best friend at the firm fired by absorbing so much of the man's work that he becomes useless. Keating knows a girl in New York named Catherine Halsey, who is plain but has a beautiful smile, and who loves Keating. Keating enjoys his time with Catherine, who he calls Katie. During one of their talks, Katie mentions that her uncle is Ellsworth Toohey, a renowned architecture critic. The revelation shocks Keating, who suddenly has a premonition that his life will be dirty and impure. He asks Katie not to introduce him to Toohey.

Henry Cameron draws on his own experience to describe the future that awaits Roark. Because Roark has integrity, Cameron says, the world will crush him. Cameron predicts that Roark will design the most beautiful building anyone has ever seen, but that the world will refuse his design. Desperate to get the project made, Roark will beg and plead, but mediocre architects will always get the commissions. Roark will break and cry like an animal. Cameron asks if Roark wants such a future, and Roark replies that he does.

SUMMARY: CHAPTER 5

Keating becomes chief designer at Francon & Heyer by getting Stengel to leave. Keating is assigned his first design job, but he is unsure of himself, and he takes his sketches to Roark. Roark takes Keating's jumbled designs and reworks them to give them unity and grace. Ashamed but grateful, Keating takes Roark's sketches and calls them his own.

ANALYSIS: CHAPTERS 1–5

Ayn Rand admitted that she was mainly interested in using her novels to convey her philosophy. She intentionally crafts simplistic prose and characters in order to avoid distraction and keep the focus on her philosophy. She writes simple sentences, and does not use figures of speech that most writers use. This stark style makes her sentences sound didactic or instructional rather than entertaining. Like the novel's protagonist, Roark, the language of *The Fountainhead* is absolute and unwavering. Rand portrays her characters' qualities very bluntly so that we can evaluate the characters accurately from the outset, and we become aware of her feelings toward them as soon as she introduces them. In short, she presents the world as basically black and white—composed of those, like Roark, who subscribe to her philosophy and those, like Keating, who don't.

The four men whose names serve as the titles for the four parts of *The Fountainhead*—Peter Keating, Ellsworth Toohey, Gail Wynand, and Howard Roark—are the main characters of the novel, but Roark is the undisputed protagonist. While in each part the omniscient narrator focuses on the individual after whom that part is named, Roark remains a fundamental presence in all of them. Thus Keating, Toohey, and Wynand function as either Roark's rivals or his foils (a foil is a literary character whose attitudes or emotions contrast with, and thereby accentuate, those of another character). The superficial similarities between Roark and these men serve first to emphasize the fundamental differences between him and them and second to give us a clearer idea of Roark's character. Each of these characters represents one value or belief. Roark, for example, stands for inspirational strength, and follows his convictions without ever weakening. Keating, on the other hand, serves as a foil for Roark. He stands for plagiarism and sycophantism. Roark's self-confidence and lack of concern for what others think of him contrast with Keating's insecurity and desire for praise, a contrast that drives much of the novel.

The first five chapters illustrate Roark's and Keating's personalities, underscoring the great difference between the two men. Rand makes it obvious that their different personalities do not arise from a difference in their recent circumstances by starting them off at exactly the same point. At the beginning of the novel Roark and Keating attend the same school, work in the same field, and move to New York at the same time. Rand presents Roark as a natural being, his own man. We first see Roark standing naked among granite cliffs, which suggests that he is as clean and pure as the elements that surround him. Rand presents Keating, in contrast, as self-absorbed and unable to think for himself. We first see Keating wrapped in a graduation robe, constantly reevaluating himself based on the opinions of others. Whereas Roark thrills to a future he will carve out himself, Keating lacks the ability to plan his own future. *The Fountainhead* alternates between scenes of Roark's moral success and financial failure and Keating's moral failure and financial success.

Foreshadowing fills the first five chapters of *The Fountainhead*. Rand uses Roark's and Keating's employers to suggest what her main characters will become. Like Keating, Francon is a fake who takes credit for the work of others and enjoys great economic and social success. Like Roark, Cameron is strong, stubborn and idealistic. Cameron even likens himself to Roark, and warns Roark that the conservative world will crush Roark just as it crushed Cameron years before. Right away we get the impression that Francon and Cameron are the older counterparts of Roark and Keating.

PART I: CHAPTERS 6–10

SUMMARY: CHAPTER 6
In January of 1925, Ellsworth M. Toohey publishes his history of architecture, *Sermons in Stone*. The book is an overnight success. A month later, Henry Cameron collapses in his office, overwhelmed by the loss of an important commission. Cameron's sister takes him back to New Jersey. At Cameron's request, Roark closes the office and burns every sketch. Meanwhile, Peter Keating, who still works at Francon & Heyer, has become very successful. He lives in a modest but stylish apartment off posh Park Avenue. Against his wishes, his controlling mother has come to live with him and help him on his way up. She suggests that Keating get close to Francon's daughter, but Francon has no interest in introducing them. Keating goes to see Katie and suddenly asks her if they are engaged. Katie understands this question as a proposal and says that they are engaged. Keating asks that they keep their engagement a secret.

SUMMARY: CHAPTER 7
Keating asks Francon to hire Roark, and Francon does so. In need of money, Roark accepts Keating's offer on the condition that he not do any designing work. Keating takes a certain sadistic pleasure in giving Roark orders, but Roark's quiet obedience frustrates him. In secret, Keating continues to ask Roark for help with his designs. Roark is happiest on the days when he goes to inspect building sites. He surprises the workers with his familiarity with construction. On

one job site, Roark befriends a worker named Mike, a tough electrician who appreciates skill of every kind.

SUMMARY: CHAPTER 8

One day Francon asks Roark to design a building based on the Dana building, one of Cameron's most successful projects. Francon suggests a derivative of the Dana building done in Classical Greek style. Roark says it would be more true to Cameron's spirit to do something innovative. Roark's pleas offend Francon, who is unused to refusal from subordinates. He promptly fires Roark. Roark begins searching for a new job, but none of the firms he speaks to are interested in him.

SUMMARY: CHAPTER 9

Roark finds work at the firm of an architect named John Erik Snyte. Every designer at Snyte's firm draws each project from a different historical perspective, and Snyte combines their plans for the final drawing. Snyte designates Roark Mr. Modernistic.

The building-trades unions of New York go on strike to demand higher wages. The most vocal antiunion papers are those owned by the media magnate Gail Wynand. Ellsworth Toohey is expected to address the strikers. He supports the striking workers, but has never publicly said so; he has a column in the *Banner,* one of Wynand's papers, and to support the strikers would end his career in journalism.

Katie no longer pays exclusive attention to Keating, which upsets Keating. He shows up at the rally and has almost persuaded Katie to leave when Toohey begins to speak hypnotically and powerfully. Even Keating falls under Toohey's spell as he speaks of unity and selflessness. Nonetheless, Keating still urges Katie to leave as she appears completely enraptured by her uncle's voice. The day after the big meeting, Wynand gives Toohey a substantial raise, insisting it is not a bribe to keep Toohey quiet. The strike is settled. One day Keating finds Francon in a miserable mood. His daughter, Dominique, has written a biting indictment of one of Francon's buildings in her column in the *Banner.*

SUMMARY: CHAPTER 10

At an elite New York society party, Francon finally introduces Keating to his daughter. Keating amuses her and they banter, but she eventually snubs him. A man named Austen Heller hires Snyte's firm to design a house for him. Heller cannot describe exactly what he wants, but no other firm has been able to satisfy his desire for a pure, distinctive building. The project excites Roark, and he shapes his design around the granite cliff on which the house will stand. Snyte gives Heller a plan that is an altered version of Roark's building. Heller says the plan is close, but he wants more purity in the design. When Roark steps forward and writes all over the final design, Snyte and the other designers are too shocked to interfere. Roark's original design emerges. Snyte fires him on the spot, but Heller is impressed and privately gives Roark the commission. He makes out the first check to "Howard Roark, Architect."

ANALYSIS: CHAPTERS 6–10

Rand labels each new character strong or weak, measuring each against the epitome of strength, Roark. Rand assigns her characters to one group or the other based on their opinions of Roark. Weak people are also those who cannot understand Roark's refusal to conform, and Rand portrays them as a despicable group. Most of the weak are affable, like Keating and Toohey, but their smiles are dishonest and they simultaneously depend on and loathe Roark for his talent. Strong people, on the other hand, admire and respect Roark. Cameron, Mike, and Heller fall into this category, and each makes an almost instantaneous connection with him. Both Heller and Mike become keenly aware of Roark's abilities although they hardly interact with him, as if one instant is sufficient time to grasp Roark's genius. Roark's profound genius and power blaze forth even in the most insignificant conversations. Every new character in the novel eventually encounters Roark, and each character's initial reaction to Roark provides a reliable indicator of how Rand values that character.

Roark's nemesis, Ellsworth Monkton Toohey, appears only briefly in these early chapters, but already his talent for persuasion makes him a powerful figure. We see Toohey's persuasiveness in his hypnotic speech at the union meeting and in his skillfully written history of architecture. In both speaking and writing, Toohey tries not to change people's minds but to empty them and then plant his own ideas in the vacuum. Toohey presents a friendly surface compared to Roark's cold genius, but Toohey uses his charm for evil. Toohey voices the theories of socialism and communism, ideologies that Rand hates. His speech about cooperation and unity should appeal to us, but instead it feels manipulative and oppressive. The people come together to hear their leader speak, but Rand presents their unity as slavery, not cooperation, as if the people are prisoners of Toohey's voice.

Dominique Francon, the first and only strong woman we encounter in The Fountainhead, closely resembles Roark. She contrasts with the other female characters, who are either manipulative and stifling like Mrs. Keating or sweet and weak-willed like Katie. Aside from Dominique, all of the female characters are superficial New York socialites who gossip or shop. Dominique is different. Rand likens her body to one of Roark's drawings. She has the signature Roark elements of elegance: angles, coldness, and poise. Like Roark's severe architectural designs, she is stern and masculine, with a severely slim frame and a "vicious mouth." However, while Dominique shares Roark's opinions and aesthetics, she does not have his talent or strength, and therefore she is not his equal. Unlike Roark, Dominique has no grand passion or mission. While she recognizes beauty and genius, and writes about it, she does not create it as Roark does. Also, Roark's frigidity and indifference come from his firm conviction, but Dominique's come from her neuroses. In her experience the world destroys beauty and purity, and she tries to stay removed from the world by refraining from desire or creativity.

Roark's work on the house for Austen Heller epitomizes the difference between the pureness of his architectural designs and the forced nature of the architectural designs of those in the corporate world. Whereas Roark envisions buildings from an organic point of view, seeking to let each building express itself naturally and dictate the style in which it should be built, the corporate architects with whom Roark interacts attempt to impose superficial stylistic concerns upon buildings without any regard for each building's essential aesthetic needs. Just as Francon urges Roark to design a Classical Greek rip-off of the Dana building and discourages him from being innovative, so do the architects at John Erik Snyte's firm, each of whom must force his designs to fit a specific school of architecture. These architects work from a purely technical point of view, and the principles they apply so rigidly to their designs constrain expression and emotion and thus prevent the buildings from being truly beautiful. Roark, on the other hand, goes into a design without any preconceived notions as to how a particular building should look. Rather, he takes into account the function of the building and the environment around the proposed building site—in the case of the Heller house the granite cliff—and lets these elements organically determine how the building should look.

PART I: CHAPTERS 11–13

SUMMARY: CHAPTER 11

Howard Roark opens his own office. As soon as he signs his contract with Austen Heller, Roark goes to see Henry Cameron. Cameron feels vindicated when he sees a snapshot of Roark's office. The first visitor to Roark's new office is Peter Keating, who loudly praises Roark for his courage and inwardly resents Roark. One day, Roark sees his old friend Mike, the electrician, at work on the Heller job site. It surprises Roark that Mike is working on such a small project, but Mike says he would never miss Roark's first building. Roark constantly visits the building site, as does Austen Heller, and the two become close friends. When the Heller house is completed, it receives little notice.

SUMMARY: CHAPTER 12

Alvah Scarret, the editor-in-chief of the *Banner,* assigns Dominique Francon to investigate living conditions in the New York slums. Dominique lives in a tenement for two weeks and writes a brilliant article. Back in affluent environs, she insults wealthy landowners by describing the brutal conditions of the tenements they own. She also shocks a group of social workers by describing the laziness and greed of the tenement people she encountered. Alvah is baffled by Dominique's disregard for propriety and her fiercely neutral nature. Keating tries and fails to see Dominique again. Francon arranges for them to meet, and they converse pleasantly. Although he fears Dominique, Keating starts falling in love with her and sees her often. Late one night, a frightened Katie comes to see Keating. She has suddenly become terrified of her uncle Toohey, with whom she shares a home. Katie asks Peter to marry her the next day. Keating agrees, but as soon as Katie leaves, Mrs. Keating starts scolding and manipulating Keating, arguing that he should marry Dominique and solidify his place at Francon's firm. Keating finally agrees to put off his marriage and tells Katie of his decision the following morning. Katie loyally accepts his decision, but after their conversation they both have a strange feeling that they have missed an important chance that will not come again.

SUMMARY: CHAPTER 13

A young entrepreneur who admires Heller's house hires Roark to design a gas station. Every subsequent customer who approaches

Roark wants things done in some past style, but Roark patiently explains that he only builds according to his beliefs. He believes that the building's context should determine its form. Roark receives a commission from Whitford Sanborn, a former customer of Henry Cameron's who wants a new country home. Sanborn originally wanted Cameron to design the house, but the retired Cameron recommended Roark. Although Roark's preliminary sketches please Sanborn, his wife raises objections. Whitford Sanborn tries to compromise with Roark, but Roark refuses. Roark ultimately designs the house the way he wants, but Mrs. Sanborn refuses to live in it.

ANALYSIS: CHAPTERS 11–13

Both Roark and Keating face a number of crucial career choices in these and subsequent chapters. Rand uses such choices or trials to fine-tune her characters and reveal their true nature. Rand does not stop at stating that Roark is a determined, independent individual. She illustrates and proves his strength step-by-step by showing us how he interacts with his circumstances. When Roark must decide between compromising the design of Whitford Sanborn's country home and losing the commission, he courageously opts to preserve the integrity of his work. Similarly Roark never asks his friends to do anything for him. Mike respects Roark enough to work for him without being asked and Cameron recommends Roark to his clients blindly. All of Roark's clients approach him because they recognize the beauty of his work. Their interest is a response to his creative capacity, not to social connections or popular influence. Roark knows immediately the kind of men that will hire him: hardworking, uncompromising men who treasure their lives and business. Through all the ups and downs, Roark remains constant, focused and calm. At no point does he regret his actions or fear failure.

Keating, on the other hand, is motivated by a desperate need for approval. He wants Francon, Dominique, and his mother to think well of him and frequently plans his actions around their opinions. In Chapter 12, Keating abandons Katie in an effort to please his mother. Weak as he is himself, Keating cannot save the weak young Katie from her powerful uncle. We now see that Keating is not just spiteful and bumbling but also hurtful. His weakness leads to heartbreak. In contrast, Roark cares nothing for the opinions of others. Roark does not mind that others ignore his design of the Heller house. His insistence on doing his own work for Heller has already cost him his job at the Snyte firm, and now his own work goes unnoticed, but to Roark the loss of a job and the lack of recognition mean nothing. He cares only for the purity of the work.

Like Roark, Dominique speaks her mind with no regard for the opinion of her audience. After writing her report on the slums, her uncompromising attitude and refusal to identify herself with one camp or another parallels Roark's self-possessed withdrawal from society. Dominique presents her view of the tenement situation as matter-of-factly as Roark shows customers his sketches, even though her frankness means that she offends both the landlords and the social workers. She could please the landlords by telling them what she tells the social workers, and vice versa, but it amuses her to annoy people with unpleasant truths.

Katie's sudden fear of Toohey may seem at first to be tangential to the concerns of this section, for the important outcome of her fear is the revelation of Keating's heartlessness. Her fear is not irrelevant, however, but an expression of Rand's carefully designed plot, in which every detail has a purpose and each small incident points to future events. Katie's sudden panic about her uncle points to events that unfold only much later in the novel. Rand uses this kind of foreshadowing to ensure that we immediately understand the consequences of cowardly and selfless behavior. She wants us to understand that bad things will happen because Keating the coward refuses to heed Katie's cry for help, and because Katie the selfless goes along with Keating's decision not to marry her right away. Even though punishment does not always happen immediately, Rand drops dark hints that it will come eventually.

PART I: CHAPTERS 14–15

SUMMARY: CHAPTER 14

Cosmo-Slotnick Pictures plans to build an enormous skyscraper and holds an international competition to select an architect. Francon encourages Keating to submit a design in the firm's name. Keating knows his messy design cannot win the contest. Shamefaced, he goes to see Roark, who works all night reshaping Keating's design. After months without work, Roark's money begins to run out. One day, Cameron's sister tells Roark that Cameron is dying. Roark hurries to New Jersey to see Cameron. As he dies, Cameron tells Roark to ignore his earlier warnings and pursue his goals without ever compromising.

Keating asks Katie if they can put off their marriage until the results of the Cosmo-Slotnick competition arrive. If Keating wins, he will become a partner in the firm and win a secure salary. Keating spends most of his time with Dominique and tries to kiss her one night. Indifferent to his passion, she tells him she believes herself to be completely frigid. Keating again feels panic and fear but remembers Dominique is Francon's daughter and asks her to marry him. The proposal surprises Dominique, but she promises him seriously that she will marry him if she ever needs to punish herself.

SUMMARY: CHAPTER 15

Keating grows anxious about the outcome of the Cosmo-Slotnick competition. Lucius Heyer is dying, and his position at Francon & Heyer will soon become vacant. If Keating does not win the competition, Francon may decide to offer the partnership to someone else. Keating has evidence that Heyer once inflated construction estimates and goes to Heyer's home to blackmail him into retiring before the results of the competition are announced. While begging Keating not to expose him, Heyer suffers a second stroke and dies. To his shock, Keating discovers that deep inside he wanted to kill Heyer. A few days later, Keating discovers that Heyer left him his entire estate and that he has won the Cosmo-Slotnick competition.

Keating becomes an overnight celebrity, but frets over the fact that Dominique despises him and that Roark actually created the prizewinning design. After Dominique leaves to spend the summer at her home in Connecticut, Keating decides to go see the penniless Roark. When Keating arrives, Roark is waiting for a phone call from a bank, which is his only prospective project. Keating writes Roark a check for five hundred dollars to keep quiet about his help on the Cosmo-Slotnick building. Roark returns the check on the condition that Keating never mention Roark's involvement with such a mediocre structure. Keating reels at this insult and breaks down. Before Keating leaves, he vows to break Roark. A few days later, the bank that is Roark's only potential customer tells him that they will hire him to design a simple Greek façade in keeping with its image as a sound financial institution. Roark refuses to compromise and refuses the contract, even though it means shutting down his office. Roark asks Mike for a job and Mike refers him to a granite quarry in Connecticut.

ANALYSIS: CHAPTERS 14–15

With each decision they make, Roark and Keating solidify their personalities and walk farther down the paths they have chosen. Rand sets up a particularly sharp contrast between the two men by putting them in identical situations, setting them down by the bedside of dying men who are also their architectural elders. Roark rushes to the dying man he respects. From his deathbed, Cameron confirms all of Roark's most deeply felt beliefs. In complete contrast, Keating rushes to the bed of a dying man in order to threaten him with humiliation. His cruelty kills Heyer, and Keating understands his own murderous impulses for the first time.

We already know that by nature Roark is determined and independent, and he demonstrates that his nature cannot be swayed by adversity. He confirms his strength by refusing to compromise his principles no matter what the cost. In a particularly impressive gesture, Roark rejects the bank commission even though it means sacrificing his business. His rejection of the commission is all the more striking in that the commission would have required only a small compromise. The other clients Roark refuses differ fundamentally from his vision, but the bankers request only a small change in his design. While Roark reveals the extent of his strength, Keating reveals the extent of his repellant personality. Keating combines seemingly irreconcilable character flaws. He is at once the cringing mama's boy who cannot think for himself and the murderous bully who kills Heyer with his scare tactics. Keating becomes more loathsome with every appearance.

While Keating lusts for recognition, Roark abhors it. Keating wants to become partner in the firm not because he craves money or power, but because he thinks this position will make others look on him as a genius. In contrast, Roark makes a point of avoiding recognition. Although Mike works on Roark's houses and Cameron and Heller recommend him to clients, Roark never solicits these kindnesses. Roark knows that the kind of men who admire him are, like him, hardworking and uncompromising. They would not appreciate pandering even if he were inclined to pander.

Dominique has elements of both Keating and Roark, as her frigidity shows. Dominique accepts Keating's advances with stoicism. She does not resist him despite her clear lack of interest. The world interests Dominique so little that passing judgment or mustering a strong opinion seems strange to her. Like Roark, she reacts with bored dispassion to personal encounters that would provoke rage, misery, or embarrassment in most people. Dominique is frigid because she has never experienced truly arousing passion. In this respect, she resembles Keating, who does not know what he wants from life because he has never had any experiences worth mentioning.

PART II: CHAPTERS 1–5

SUMMARY: CHAPTER 1
Howard Roark finds hard but satisfying work at the Francon granite quarry. Dominique lives alone on her father's estate, a few miles from the quarry. She spends most of her time walking through the countryside. On one particularly hot day she visits her father's quarry. There she sees Roark drilling away at the rock. Their eyes meet and his gaze is one of ownership. She immediately hates him because she knows she could fall in love with him. Later, Dominique fights the desire to visit the quarry again but cannot help herself. Roark looks at her with the same intense gaze. Several days later, they meet at the quarry. Their first real encounter is intimate. Dominique wants to know that Roark suffers and asks him if the work is tiresome. Roark tells her that sometimes he cannot move his arms at night. Dominique asks him why he works there and he replies that he is there for the money she pays him.

SUMMARY: CHAPTER 2
Every day, Dominique fights the compulsion to visit Roark. She eventually begins to feel safe in her house, but wants to test her resolve. Dominique makes a long scratch in the marble fireplace and hires Roark to repair the damage. He casually agrees to come, making her weak with shame and pleasure. When Roark arrives at Dominique's house, he splits the marble and offers to order a new piece of stone. When the marble arrives, Dominique sends for Roark, but he sends an old laborer in his place. Later, at the quarry, Dominique asks Roark why he sent the other worker, and he wonders why she cares. Three evenings later, Dominique is sitting in her bedroom when Roark enters. He takes her in his arms roughly. She fights him, but he overpowers her. Roark then rapes her like "a master taking shameful, contemptuous possession" of a slave. Dominique realizes that this humiliation is exactly what she wants and that if Roark had behaved tenderly, she would have remained cold. Roark leaves without a word.

A week later, an industrialist named Roger Enright hires Roark and Roark leaves for New York. When Dominique discovers that Roark has left, she feels relief that she is no longer vulnerable, and reasons that she will never see him again.

SUMMARY: CHAPTER 3

Peter Keating is enjoying his newfound success when he receives an envelope from Ellsworth Toohey. Inside the envelope is a draft of Toohey's next column, a dazzling tribute to Keating and his work. Toohey also encloses a request for a meeting with Keating. Later that day, Keating learns that a sculptor named Stephen Mallory has tried to kill Toohey. Keating's first reaction to this news is to wonder whether Toohey's article will still be published. The attack leaves Toohey uninjured. Keating visits Toohey as soon as he can. A thin, narrow-chested, fragile little man, Toohey is not at all what Keating expected, but the two men get along well. Toohey asks Keating to join an informal group of young architects Toohey is putting together. He tells Keating that the group will meet once in a while to share ideas, and that Keating can be chairman.

SUMMARY: CHAPTER 4

Toohey invites Keating to tea. Katie is there, but she sits silently staring into space. Toohey interrogates Keating about Roark, even though Toohey has never mentioned Roark in his column. Toohey also arranges a commission for Keating. Lois Cook, a fashionable author who writes complicated but empty books, wants to build the ugliest house in New York. Keating accepts the project.

SUMMARY: CHAPTER 5

Dominique returns to New York. She is at work at the *Banner* when Toohey visits her. He notices a picture of the Enright House on her desk. She tells him that an architect who could conceive such a beautiful thing should never allow it to be erected for people to ruin. She adds that the building is too good for men like Toohey. The Council of American Builders, Toohey's group of architects, has a first meeting. Of its eighteen members, only two are distinguished. The members denounce the state of modern architecture but offer no suggestions for improvement. Toohey delivers a melodramatic speech that Dominique interrupts. The council members feel uncomfortable in her presence. After the meeting, Keating tries to kiss Dominique, but his advances repulse

her. He demands to know whom she has met. She tells him about
the workman in Connecticut.

ANALYSIS: CHAPTERS 1–5

In these chapters, Rand begins to reveal more of Dominique's moti-
vations and nature. Dominique is a masochist who refuses to let herself become attached to anything or anyone and lives her life amidst
the very things that torture her. She loathes society specifically
because she so passionately believes in human perfection and views
society as a threat to this perfection. She has a great appreciation for
what is pure, beautiful, and strong, and she firmly believes that the
world destroys all that is good. This sentiment grips her so strongly
that she would rather break a perfect vase than see it used by the
unworthy. All around her she finds men without character and men
who borrow their beliefs and principles from others. She hates such
men not because of their failings but because she sees them ruin the
world, and she thus lives her life in a cold, spiteful way. She refuses
to love anyone or anything for fear that the world will destroy what
she loves, and she surrounds herself with those people she likes the
least, knowing that she will be in no danger of falling in love with
them. Dominique's encounter with Roark derails her loveless existence, as she finds herself caring for a man with vision and character.
True to her philosophy, she does not celebrate this turn of events.
She fears the world will destroy this good man, so she decides to
destroy him first.

Rand presents Dominique's rape as a violent but necessary
encounter—as just what Dominique needs. Her depiction of
woman as stubborn and frigid and man as masterful and healing
might shock the modern reader. It should shock, and is partly meant
to shock, but it is also not quite an act of sexual violence between
two lifelike characters. Rand shapes characters that are symbols,
not real people. Thus the coupling of Roark and Dominique is the
coupling of symbols, not the coupling of people, and the rape is
more an abstract meditation on violence and frigidity than the hid-
eous violation of a woman by a man. Roark's rape of Dominique
dramatizes the violence and force of their mental union. Although
Roark is the rapist, he is also the victim, for he cannot resist Dominique and becomes a slave to his passions. Dominique resists not
just Roark, but her own attraction to Roark. By fighting him, Dominique tries to rid herself of her desires. Neither character utters a

word during the rape, a silence that suggests the oneness of their minds and contrasts with the physicality of the encounter. Rand foreshadows the rape when Dominique first sees Roark drilling at the granite quarry and cannot stop staring at him. She resents her fascination with him and hopes that Roark will succumb to the difficulty of the task. Instead, he continues and manages to crack the rock, in a gesture symbolizing his later success at shattering Dominique's emotional wall.

Toohey's character also develops significantly in these chapters, and we see his influence and social control grow. Toohey wants to change the nature of the social soil so that men like Roark can never grow again. He destroys beauty, such as that which Roark embodies, and in its place enshrines mediocrity, such as that which Keating embodies. Once Toohey has made gods of people like Keating, the truly talented cannot compete. He tells the small circle of young architects that beauty lies in the small and the everyday. He does not encourage them to look to abstract ideals or demanding standards. He does not expect anything of them and thus they are entirely comfortable achieving nothing too large. Toohey, in his championing of the common and the average, is the antithesis of everything for which Roark stands and for which Dominique yearns: genius, independence, and perfection. In Rand's scheme of the world, a handful of men like Roark create, produce, and inspire, while a larger, swarming majority huddle together to destroy, level, and belittle. True rebellion is born in the hearts of independent men, and through his influence Toohey tries to wipe the world clean of such men. Only when genius is eradicated can someone like Toohey hold power.

PART II: CHAPTERS 6–10

SUMMARY: CHAPTER 6

With the money from the Enright commission, Roark reopens his office. He agrees to go to a cocktail party with Austen Heller when Heller mentions that Dominique will attend. When Roark enters, the party's hostess tries to talk to him, but finds him insolent. Heller introduces Roark to Dominique. She engages him in a polite conversation, and neither of them mentions their previous encounter. Dominique feels that Roark is testing her. Toohey spends the evening watching Roark carefully.

SUMMARY: CHAPTER 7

Dominique's next column attacks the Enright House, but Toohey accuses her of actually subtly praising Roark. One of Roark's potential clients, Joel Sutton, grows anxious and asks Dominique if he should hire Roark. She tells him that Roark will create a beautiful building for him, but Sutton wants something safe. Dominique recommends Keating. That night, Dominique visits Roark. She coldly states that she wants him, but that she hates him because her desire for him is so strong. She promises to do everything in her power to destroy him because she needs to test his strength. Roark understands her need and admires her.

SUMMARY: CHAPTER 8

> When they lay in bed together it was—as it had to be
> ... an act of violence. It was surrender, made the
> more complete by the force of their resistance.
> (See QUOTATIONS, p. 56)

Over the next few months, Dominique earns four commissions for Keating. Toohey visits her and proposes an alliance against Roark. She agrees. Dominique and Roark visit each other often, always at night. Dominique revels in Roark's strength and in her inability to resist him. By day, Dominique devotes her energies to destroying Roark. Roger Enright, furious with Dominique, takes her to see the unfinished Enright House. Standing within the building's frame makes Dominique euphoric. She writes an article saying no one should be allowed to live in the building. Enright is bewildered by this hidden praise of Roark. Keating cannot decipher Dominique's actions. Everyone in New York thinks that Dominique is in love with Keating, but in private she refuses to talk to him.

SUMMARY: CHAPTER 9

When Toohey was a child, he hated anyone distinctive. He tried to destroy the unique and disguised his cruelty behind words of humility. To Toohey's surprise, people believed him, and he soon had a following. At Harvard, Toohey was especially popular among wealthy heirs. As an adult, he began preaching submitting oneself to the needs of others. Upon coming to New York, he became a vocational adviser. He rarely counseled students to follow their dreams, encouraging them to pursue undesirable careers instead. Toohey then started publishing and became a celebrity.

SUMMARY: CHAPTER 10

In June of 1929, the Enright House opens. Roark receives more commissions. He signs a contract with a man named Anthony Cord to build a fifty-story skyscraper in Manhattan, his first office building. A man named Kent Lansing approaches Roark. Lansing wants Roark to design a luxurious hotel for Lansing's corporation. After weeks of vicious debating, Lansing wins over the rest of the corporation's board and they select Roark to build the Aquitania Hotel.

Hopton Stoddard, one of Toohey's dependents, wants to build a temple to religion. Toohey sees an opportunity and tells Stoddard to hire Roark. Toohey coaches Stoddard to give a speech that will win over Roark. Although Stoddard's appearance and manner disgust Roark, Stoddard's arguments impress him. Stoddard says he wants to build a temple to the human spirit and wants Roark to infuse it with his own soul. Roark thinks perhaps he does not understand people as well as he thought he did and agrees to design the temple.

ANALYSIS: CHAPTERS 6–10

Dominique and Roark's love affair demonstrates the novel's premise that real passion involves struggle and submission. Dominique admires Roark intensely and wants to protect him from the world's stupidity, but because she wants to test Roark's strength she tries to destroy him in print and rob him of his commissions. Dominique pits herself against Roark in hopes that he will foil her attempts to ruin him, which would thus disprove her cynical view of the world. Roark understands her actions perfectly, and the public antagonism between Roark and Dominique does not drive them apart, but brings them together. Dominique's attempts to crush Roark drive the normally frigid pair to a state of ecstasy.

Rand contrasts the harsh and exquisite love of Dominique and Roark with the tender cuddling of Keating and Katie. Keating and Katie always treat each other with consideration and consequently their love feels flat and devoid of real sexual charge. They also lack the intuitive understanding of one another that Dominique and Roark enjoy. Roark always understands what motivates Dominique's behavior, even when she acts in ways that most people would find perverse or inexplicable. Keating seems to misunderstand the most basic facts about Katie, not noticing, for example, that her very soul is being threatened by her uncle. Even in love affairs, *The*

Fountainhead favors the strong over the weak, praising the violence of Roark's relationship over the meekness of Keating's relationship.

Rand shows us that Toohey's lifework will never succeed. He spends his days trying to destroy the exceptional. He wants to convince the world that mediocrity is the greatest attribute, thereby robbing mankind of its idealism and ambition. However, Toohey can never destroy every genius and he can never persuade everyone to aim for mediocrity. Theoretical sympathy for the masses motivates Toohey, who sees the accomplishments of great men as insults to the millions who cannot achieve greatness in their own right. Tooley's motivation is also personal. He knows that he will never join the ranks of the elite, so instead of wasting his energy attempting to join them, he attempts to destroy them. He believes that if he can convince the world that mediocrity is the greatest of attributes, if he can rob mankind of its idealism and hope, if he can flatten all of society into a smooth mass of unexceptional men, then he can become a great man. In order to achieve his goals, Toohey employs the language and arguments of religion and socialism. Rand was both a staunch atheist and a great antisocialist. She found that both religion and socialism ask humans to renounce themselves for a greater good. Such renunciation of the ego is dangerous, argues Rand, as it opens an individual up to manipulation. She makes both of these systems unappealing to us by making them the ideals of the repellant Toohey.

PART II: CHAPTERS 11–15

SUMMARY: CHAPTER 11

> [Y]ou've gone beyond the probable and made us see
> the possible, but possible only through you. Because
> your figures are more devoid of contempt of humanity
> than any work I've ever seen.
>
> (See QUOTATIONS, p. 57)

Peter Keating is unhappy with the completed Cosmo-Slotnick building, but Toohey tells Keating to give up his ego if he wants to be great. Roark goes to find Stephen Mallory, the sculptor who tried to kill Toohey. Mallory is shocked by Roark's interest in his work and cries with relief at the knowledge that uncompromising men like Roark exist. The following morning, Mallory visits Roark and looks at the sketches for the Stoddard temple. Mallory agrees to sculpt a statue of the human spirit for the temple. Roark suggests Dominique for a model.

For the next few months, Roark works with brilliant intensity. He designs a horizontal temple, scaled to human height. He wants it to bring the sky down to man and allow visitors to find strength.

SUMMARY: CHAPTER 12

In May, the corporation backing the Aquitania Hotel falls apart and construction is suspended. Kent Lansing promises Roark that one day he will finish the Aquitania. Stoddard abruptly cancels the imminent opening of the Stoddard Temple. The next day, Toohey writes a vicious criticism of the temple and Stoddard files suit against Roark for breach of contract and malpractice. Every newspaper in the city supports Stoddard. Toohey explains to Dominique that now people will remember Roark for botching a building. At the trial, many prominent architects in New York testify against Roark. Dominique testifies on Stoddard's behalf, but actually defends Roark. She says the Stoddard Temple should be leveled because the world does not deserve it. Roark's only defense is to submit ten photographs of the Stoddard Temple.

SUMMARY: CHAPTER 13

Stoddard wins the suit. For her next column, Dominique submits her trial testimony, over Alvah Scarret's objections. Dominique threatens to quit if the article is not printed, and the paper's owner, Gail Wynand, orders Scarret to fire Dominique. Meanwhile, Katie goes to Toohey for advice. She is utterly unhappy in her job as a social worker and is beginning to hate the people she is supposed to help. Toohey tells Katie to relinquish her ego. Katie meekly agrees. Keating bitterly regrets his testimony against Roark at the Stoddard trial. He tells Katie he wants to marry her right away and that they will elope the next day. After he leaves, Katie shouts at Toohey that she is not afraid of him anymore.

SUMMARY: CHAPTER 14

The same evening, Dominique asks Keating to marry her and he accepts. They drive to Connecticut and get married. That night, Dominique goes to Roark. After they make love, Dominique tells Roark for the first time that she loves him. She then tells him that she married Keating. Roark accepts the news quietly. Dominique tells

Roark that she will punish herself by marrying Keating because she refuses to be happy in a world that does not appreciate Roark. Roark tells her that he loves her and will not stop her. He wants her whole and will wait for her to grow.

SUMMARY: CHAPTER 15
The next morning, Dominique moves into Keating's apartment. Keating's marriage is a sham, but he takes pleasure in the envy of other men. The Stoddard Temple is redesigned by a group of architects and converted into the Stoddard Home for Subnormal Children. After completing the Cord skyscraper, Roark cannot find any work. The Wall Street Crash of 1929 has nearly ruined the building trades, and no one wants to take a chance on a scandalous architect. One night Roark goes to see the altered temple. Toohey emerges, taunts Roark, and asks Roark what he thinks of him. Roark says he doesn't think of Toohey at all.

ANALYSIS : CHAPTERS 11–15
The media is the most powerful and despicable public institution in *The Fountainhead*. Although Rand published her novel before television became ubiquitous, newspapers and magazines are omnipresent in the novel and reach everybody. Toohey exploits and manipulates the media to its full extent. His mediocrity prevents him from expressing himself through his own art or architecture, but he reaches the public and hurts Roark with his column in the *Banner*. Because the media shapes opinions and knowledge, Toohey at first hurts Roark simply by failing to write about him and thus keeping him from the public eye. But Toohey must switch strategies after Roark becomes known, and he begins using his newspaper column to launch an attack on Roark's reputation.

The extent of Toohey's maliciousness becomes increasingly apparent in these chapters, as he manipulates Stoddard into hiring Roark, letting him begin the building, and then firing and suing him. Characters react to Toohey's repulsiveness in different ways. Dominique thinks the horrible world deserves Toohey and his collectivist philosophy, and so she does not try to stop him. Stephen Mallory sees Toohey as the embodiment of the world's brutal irrationality and tries to stop Toohey by shooting him. Howard Roark poses the greatest threat to Toohey and suffers the most at Toohey's hands, and he reacts with cold indifference to the crazed columnist. When

Toohey and Roark meet at Stoddard's temple, Toohey expects the meeting to be a fiery clash between two powerful enemies. Instead, Toohey finds that Roark does not even think about him. Roark thinks of Toohey not as an equal, but as a distasteful nuisance. Roark's ability to ignore Toohey confirms the latter's mediocrity.

Dominique and Keating form an unhappy union that contrasts with the idyllic marriage that earlier seems possible between Katie and Keating. Both Katie and Keating feel that they could make each other happy; Keating could protect Katie from Toohey and Katie could make Keating feel honest and pure. Yet Keating is too weak and greedy to know what is good for him. Dominique and Keating marry not to find happiness, but because Dominique wants to punish herself. She hates living in a world that does not understand Roark, and to fight successfully on Roark's behalf would mean stooping to the tactics of the world she hates. The marriage frustrates Keating, who enjoys the congratulations of his friends but fears his wife's cold indifference.

Throughout *The Fountainhead* Rand illustrates Roark's individuality and strength on conviction by highlighting his apathy toward or distaste for institutions. He gets expelled from the Stanton Institute of Technology because his designs are too modern and he is unwilling to conform to conventional standards. But this conservative reaction to his work does not faze him, and, wholly uninterested in working at a conventional design firm such as Francon & Heyer, he seeks to work for the individualistic Henry Cameron. Similarly, at the trial, in Chapter 12, Roark makes no attempt to put forth a defense that could actually win him the case. He does not care about the legal system or about triumphing in it; rather, he seeks only to defend the integrity of his work. He shows the same lack of concern for marriage; because he sees it as a meaningless formality, he feels no jealousy toward Keating about his marriage to Dominique and feels no compunction about committing adultery with her. He considers all value systems but his own utterly irrelevant.

PART III: CHAPTERS 1–4

SUMMARY: CHAPTER 1

Newspaper magnate Gail Wynand is contemplating a new real estate venture called Stoneridge. Toohey recommends Keating as the architect for Stoneridge. When Wynand is skeptical, Toohey tells Wynand he should meet Dominique Keating before deciding. Toohey also tells Wynand he has a present that will convince Wynand. Later that evening, Wynand digs into his past to find a memory that will convince him to live.

Wynand grew up in the gang-infested Hell's Kitchen section of Manhattan. He had no use for the neighborhood schools and began working as a boy at a local paper called the *Gazette*. When the *Gazette* tried to frame an honest man, Wynand turned to one of his journalistic idols for help. When his idol refused to help, Wynand began to feel contempt for men of integrity. A few years later, Wynand seized control of a local paper from a political gang. He renamed the paper the *Banner*. In its first big campaign, the paper tried to solicit money from its readers on behalf of two people: a brilliant young scientist and the pregnant girlfriend of an executed murderer. The donations for the pregnant girl overwhelmed the donations for the scientist, which indicated to Wynand what the paper should cover if he wanted it to be popular. At the age of thirty-five, Wynand owned papers across the United States.

Wynand now keeps a secret art gallery filled with masterpieces. After his meeting with Toohey, Wynand finds a large crate waiting for him. He opens it and finds Mallory's statue of Dominique inside. Wynand calls Toohey and agrees to meet Dominique.

SUMMARY: CHAPTER 2
One evening, Keating and Dominique talk. Keating observes that there is no real Dominique anymore and wonders aloud what has happened to her soul. Dominique replies by asking about Keating's soul, observing that Keating himself has no opinions of his own. Keating is about to agree when a phone call from Toohey interrupts him. Toohey says Wynand wishes to meet with Dominique to discuss Stoneridge.

SUMMARY: CHAPTER 3
When they meet, Dominique and Wynand connect instantly. Dominique, who is just as beautiful as her statue, impresses Wynand. She offers to sleep with Wynand if he will give the Stoneridge contract to Keating, but Wynand correctly guesses that Dominique only makes this offer because the thought of sleeping with him repulses her. Wynand's insight surprises Dominique. Later, Wynand meets Keating and Dominique at an elegant restaurant. Wynand tells Keating that he will give him Stoneridge in exchange for Dominique. A week later, Wynand takes Dominique to see his art collection.

SUMMARY: CHAPTER 4

Wynand and Dominique go for a long cruise on Wynand's yacht, the *I Do*. Wynand tells Dominique that when he was a child people had always told him he didn't run things, and the yacht's name is meant to contradict those people. The cruise is peaceful and comfortable. Wynand tells Dominique he is in love with her and asks her to marry him. His proposal shocks Dominique. She begins to question all of her assumptions about Wynand. When Dominique remembers the Stoddard Temple and the *Banner*'s campaign against Roark, she agrees to marry Wynand.

ANALYSIS: CHAPTERS 1–4

Wynand is the only character in *The Fountainhead* who does not fit neatly into a category, and the only truly tragic one as well. Wynand resembles Roark; both men are self-made, dynamic, and gifted. Unlike Roark, however, he became disillusioned after his early idols turned out to be shams. Like Toohey, Wynand sells himself to the public for power and devotes his life to proving his conviction that no one with true integrity actually exists. Wynand thus belongs to both Roark and Toohey's world, and Dominique has a mixed reaction to Wynand because of his dual nature. Wynand's contempt for beauty repels Dominique, but his strength attracts her. Wynand's secret art gallery suggests the tragedy of a split identity. The art gallery is Wynand's prosthetic spirit, a substitute for the private soul he gave up during his rise to power. The beauty of the works in the gallery inspires and nourishes Wynand, but also pains him. He knows that he will never put his love for beauty over his shallow public self.

Rand times Wynand's entrance into the narrative to maximize his importance to the novel's characters and events. We feel Wynand's power and influence from the beginning, but until now the man himself has not appeared. When Wynand finally enters the story, we are as surprised as Dominique to find that this shadowy figure possesses some of the virtues *The Fountainhead* idealizes. The story of Wynand's lost idealism suggests that an encounter with Roark will stir up old feelings in Wynand, especially because we see Roark's sway over other strong figures. Upon meeting Roark, the sculptor Mallory, for example, changes his mind and decides that incorruptible men do exist. Similarly, Dominique's meeting with Roark causes her to reevaluate her worldview. This evidence of Roark's power makes us anticipate an explosive first encounter between Roark and Wynand.

Keating's fireside conversation with Dominique in Chapter 2 demonstrates his ability to think honestly and purely. At times, Keating is able to understand that a void is inside him, although he never finds the strength to fill that void. Keating sees Roark's existence as an insult to his world and its standards, but he also understands Roark's greatness. Keating has always hated Roark, but this hatred is just a redirected contempt for Keating's own weakness. Although Keating does not redeem his flaws, his knowledge of his crimes and his grudging admiration of Roark make him less despicable than many of his colleagues, who remain happily ignorant of their shortcomings. Keating becomes a pitiable figure, completely overmastered by Dominique. Although Keating provokes our contempt, it seems that Dominique treats him with more cruelty than he deserves.

PART III: CHAPTERS 5–9

SUMMARY: CHAPTER 5

> *He was not the corrupt publisher of a popular empire.*
> *He was an aristocrat aboard a yacht. He looked, she*
> *thought, like what one believes an aristocrat to be when*
> *one is young: a brilliant kind of gaiety without guilt.*
> (See QUOTATIONS, p. 58)

Wynand and Dominique return to New York and Wynand goes to see Keating. He offers Keating $250,000 and the Stoneridge contract in exchange for Dominique. After a moment's hesitation, Keating accepts. Later, he feels an immense grief over his loss and realizes that he loves Dominique. Toohey dislikes the idea of a union between Dominique and Wynand, two people who are potentially very dangerous to him. Dominique goes to visit Roark, who is now working at a construction site in Clayton, Ohio. She finds him working late and tells him her plans. Roark remembers that Henry Cameron hated Wynand. Dominique's news pains Roark, but he does not object. He and Dominique talk with an easy intimacy, but their time together is very painful for her.

SUMMARY: CHAPTER 6

Ike, a member of Toohey's new Council of American Writers, reads his play at an informal meeting. The play is awful, but like Toohey's young architects, the young writers congratulate each other on their mediocre talent. With Toohey's help, they have become the nation's literary elite. In his column, Toohey comes out in support of modern architecture. In Europe, more and more architects are designing pale imitations of Henry Cameron's buildings, and Toohey approves of this trend. Modern architecture, he argues, is now a cohesive and organized style. This change in tastes hurts Keating, whose works are all combinations of other styles. Francon retires and Keating picks a lazy designer named Neil Dumont as his new partner. The firm begins to slip.

SUMMARY: CHAPTER 7

When Dominique returns to New York, Wynand wants a quick, private ceremony. Dominique, however, wants a huge public wedding, as crass and vulgar as possible. They get married in an elaborate ceremony at an exclusive hotel and Dominique wears a long black dress. The *Banner* is flooded with letters denouncing Wynand's marriage to a divorced and decadent woman.

SUMMARY: CHAPTER 8

Wynand and Dominique don't leave their penthouse for two weeks. Although Dominique never forgets that Wynand represents everything evil in the world, she finds his heart and soul somehow heroic. Whenever Dominique asks about Wynand's newspapers, he coldly responds that he will never apologize for the *Banner*. In the spring, Wynand leaves for a publisher's convention. When he returns, Dominique brings him to see the play of one of Toohey's protégées, which the *Banner* has highly praised. Dominique forces Wynand to face the world he created. She calls them both traitors—herself for sacrificing happiness in order to escape the world, and Wynand for sacrificing his integrity in order to control it. Wynand admits that he hates the idea of perfection. There is no such thing as a perfectly honorable man, he claims, and he has spent a great deal of money and time trying to prove it.

SUMMARY: CHAPTER 9

Wynand tells Dominique that he plans to erect a building of great beauty in Hell's Kitchen. Dominique warns Wynand about Toohey, who has slowly replaced much of the staff of the *Banner* with his favorites. Dominique says that Wynand is trying to assume control of the paper so that he can control the world. Wynand only laughs at her warning. At times, Wynand and Dominique barely speak. When

Wynand tells Dominique that he loves her, she thinks of Roark. Dominique apologizes to Wynand for marrying him but not loving him. Wynand does not care and replies that he is happy. He has never loved anything before and she gives his life meaning.

ANALYSIS: CHAPTERS 5–9

In these chapters Toohey's small efforts start to accumulate and gain momentum, and Rand likens Toohey's machinations to events following the Russian Revolution of 1917. Toohey begins to grow more powerful in a series of moves that mimic the rise of Russian dictator Joseph Stalin in the 1920s. Stalin worked to replace all the men in the lowly positions in the Communist party. When elections came, Stalin's opponent Trotsky found himself ousted by a party of Stalin loyalists. Once Stalin came to power, he eliminated great numbers of able and distinguished men so that no one could challenge him. Similarly, Toohey tries to create a world where men like Roark and Mallory are not only ignored but actively destroyed. Toohey's followers and protégées increase in number, and although they are all substandard men, they become very prominent with the support of a sensationalist press controlled by Toohey. As Dominique realizes, Toohey has begun weeding out the talented people from Wynand's staff and replacing them with his own mediocre people. Although Wynand is officially the boss, Toohey slowly attacks Wynand's base of power and even turns the newspaper staff against Wynand.

Keating's cynical decision to sell his wife to Wynand marks the end of his brief happiness, and with this display of weakness and amorality his fortunes begin to change. In only a few chapters, Keating gives up a woman he loves, finds that Toohey no longer has time for him, and enters a period of mediocrity unusual even for him. Early in the novel, Keating's and Roark's careers were juxtaposed, but now Keating is never mentioned in the same breath with Roark's name. Toohey, who built Keating's career by praising him in the newspaper, now distances himself from his protégé by embracing a philosophy of architecture that contradicts everything Keating has ever designed. Consistent with his philosophy, Toohey thinks of Keating not as a human being, but as a pawn that must move wherever Toohey's whim commands. Keating can no longer rely on Katie, for she has capitulated to her uncle and become a broken woman. Keating has always drawn his strength from the praise and loyalty of others, and once they leave him he finds himself with no inner resources.

Wynand, on the other hand, regains the convictions of his youth and becomes stronger as Dominique's influence begins to chip away at his disillusionment. Although Dominique never gets Wynand to express regret for his misdeeds, she does make him reconsider his actions, and leaves him primed to come over to Roark's side. She helps pull Wynand's true heart and spirit from beneath the ruthlessness and forcefulness that mark his way of doing business.

PART IV: CHAPTERS 1-5

SUMMARY: CHAPTER 1

In 1935, a young man who is discouraged by life bicycles through the woods. He sees a resort designed by Howard Roark, and its design gives him enough courage to last a lifetime.

We learn the story of how Roark came to design this resort: Roark hears of a group of developers hoping to build a resort in Monadnock Valley for people of moderate income. Roark does not think the board will give him the project, but he goes to see them. He argues that resorts should make people feel sheltered and unique. To his surprise, the board gives him the commission. They are almost too eager to be true, but Roark's work so engrosses him that he hardly notices. He employs all his old allies, including Stephen Mallory. They live idyllically together in shacks in the valley. As the opening date approaches, it seems as if the company wants to keep customers away, but people still rent every house in Monadnock Valley. It turns out that the developers were hoping to cheat their investors by making the resort fail, and picked Roark because they thought he was a bad architect. This angers Mallory, but Roark reminds him that none of it matters because the resort has been built.

In 1936, Roark receives a call from Wynand asking for a meeting.

SUMMARY: CHAPTER 2

Wynand and Roark immediately connect with one another. Wynand does not know about Roark and Dominique's affair and Dominique does not know the two men are meeting. Wynand asks Roark to design him a private home. Some buildings, says Wynand, are cheap showoffs, but Roark's buildings all share a sense of joy. Roark is surprised that Wynand understands him so completely. Wynand says he wants the house to be a fortress that shields his wife from the world.

Roark accepts the project. After Roark leaves, Wynand reads every article the *Banner* has ever printed about Roark.

SUMMARY: CHAPTER 3
Wynand and Roark walk for hours on the proposed site of Wynand's house. They discuss their similarities, and how both overcame tough circumstances and achieved success. Roark does not nurse any grudges over the *Banner*'s earlier criticism of him. After completing the initial sketches, Roark visits Wynand's office. Wynand tells Roark he will only build the house if Roark agrees to become Wynand's personal architect and design all future buildings in whatever style Wynand wants. If Roark refuses, Wynand will destroy him. Roark makes a quick sketch of a traditional house and asks Wynand if that is what he wants. Wynand recoils from the drawing, and Roark tells Wynand not to bother him with orders or suggestions. Wynand laughs because this is proof that Roark is a truly incorruptible man.

SUMMARY: CHAPTER 4
Wynand shows Roark's drawings to Dominique without telling her who drew them. Dominique recognizes that the house was designed as tribute to Roark's love for her. Roark arrives at their apartment and he and Dominique act as if nothing has happened between them. Dominique sees the familiarity between Wynand and Roark and realizes that Roark's purity has led to Wynand's redemption. Later, Wynand calls Toohey to his office and forbids him from ever mentioning Roark's name in his column. Toohey agrees.

SUMMARY: CHAPTER 5
Wynand begins to feel disgusted when he is at work. Whenever this happens, Wynand telephones Roark and asks to see him. Meanwhile, it tortures Dominique to know that Roark is so close to her and yet impossible to reach. She understands that Roark is still testing her. She tells herself over and over again that she would do anything for him.

ANALYSIS: CHAPTERS 1–5
Keating's weakness has made him fade in importance, and Wynand takes over Keating's earlier role as a foil for Roark. Wynand's presence clarifies the novel's definition of strength as a quality that comes from independence, not power and dominance. Roark has

true strength, and Wynand does not. Rand emphasizes that the men themselves, not circumstances, shaped their personalities. She gives the men the same background to argue that if Roark could transcend his early years, then Wynand could have done the same. Like Keating, Wynand comes from a poor family, makes his own fortune, and understands the importance of beauty and integrity. But whereas Roark chooses to ignore the corrupt outside world, Wynand lowers himself to the level of that world, grabbing as much power and control as he can. Neither man wants to compromise, but Roark correctly believes that even small compromises corrupt a man. Wynand mistakenly believes that compromising along the way is acceptable, for he aims to win so much power that he will never again have to compromise. Wynand does not understand that strength lies in independence and self-reliance, not control.

When Wynand and Roark finally meet, Wynand immediately recognizes that Roark completes him. He decides he must redeem himself by changing his relationship with the world. Like Dominique, Wynand first tests Roark by trying to corrupt him, offering him work on condition that Roark relinquish artistic control. Once Roark passes the test by refusing the offer, Wynand realizes that Roark is a truly principled man. Wynand had founded his cynical worldview on the idea that incorruptible men like Roark do not exist, so when Roark resists Wynand's offers and threats, Wynand has to change his worldview. Although Wynand welcomes the change, he finds it difficult to enact, for it involves dismantling the ugliness Wynand has spent a lifetime creating.

Toohey's influence spreads and grows, but the power of Roark's work intensifies, which suggests Rand's belief that art can combat evil. Roark's work begins to attract a national audience. The Monadnock resort is a triumph for Roark, for despite the fact that the project is set up specifically to fail, he manages to create a place of beauty that people love instinctively. Roark reaches both the masses and individuals through his work. Rand believes that art saves souls and lives, and, in Part IV, Chapter 1, his Monadnock resort does indeed save a young man. This young man feels alienated and resigned to a lifetime of desperation and need, but a simple glimpse of Monadnock rejuvenates his spirit. Rand wants to bring solace to readers with *The Fountainhead* just as Roark brings solace to the young man with his resort complex. *The Fountainhead* is an anthem for the indestructible spirit of humankind. Roark embodies the joy and spirit of humankind and his creations are proof that perfection is possible in this messy world.

PART IV: CHAPTERS 6–10

SUMMARY: CHAPTER 6

> *I've been a parasite all my life. . . . I have fed on you
> and all the men like you who lived before we were
> born. . . . I have taken that which was not mine and
> given nothing in return.*
>
> (See QUOTATIONS, p. 59)

Ellsworth Toohey attends a dinner party hosted by a petulant heir with no talents of his own. The guests at the party all speak as if they were Toohey's puppets. The guests revile Wynand and argue that unselfishness is the only true virtue. After the party, Toohey walks home in a daze of exhilaration.

SUMMARY: CHAPTER 7

After Francon retires, Keating gains a reputation for being too old-fashioned. Keating puts on weight and becomes dejected and bitter. At thirty-nine, he feels lost. On weekends, Keating goes to a shack in the woods and paints, which brings him some peace but no pleasure. Keating's last professional chance lies in securing a contract for a large housing project called Cortlandt Homes. Keating asks Toohey to recommend him to the Cortlandt committee, but Toohey receives him coldly. Keating asks why Toohey has abandoned him and taken on a new favorite, named Gus Webb. Toohey replies that he only backed Keating in order to prevent the rise of truly talented men. Toohey then tells Keating that Cortlandt Homes is an architectural challenge because it must be cheap to build and easy to maintain. If Keating can overcome this challenge, Toohey says, he will back Keating. Keating knows that the design is too complicated for him and telephones Roark.

SUMMARY: CHAPTER 8

For the first time in years, Keating talks to Roark simply and honestly. They discuss the Cortlandt project, and Roark asks Keating to return to Roark's office the next day for an answer. The next day, Roark says that he will do the project because it is a puzzle he wants to solve, and not because of money or pity. Roark agrees to let Keating take credit for the plans as long as Keating does not change anything in the design. Keating vows to fight for Roark's plans, even though he knows it will be difficult. Keating realizes that although he will get the credit and the money, Roark will get the pure joy of designing a perfect building. It pleases Roark that Keating finally understands which reward is more valuable. Keating shows Roark his paintings, which he has never shown anyone else, and Roark gently tells Keating it is too late. After Keating leaves, Roark feels sick with pity and disgusted that society considers pity good.

SUMMARY: CHAPTER 9
Roark creates a design that would make the Cortlandt Homes economical as well as airy, beautiful, and functional. When Toohey sees the drawings, he declares Keating a genius, although he knows Keating did not do the designs. Gail Wynand orders every department in the *Banner* to promote Roark, but Wynand's support works against Roark. The city's intellectuals scorn the paper and anything it supports, including Roark. Wynand ignores them and continues his crusade, using his influence to win commissions for Roark. One day, Wynand takes Roark to his old Hell's Kitchen neighborhood. He plans to build a great skyscraper on the site, and wants Roark to begin dreaming about the building with him.

SUMMARY: CHAPTER 10
Keating is walking home one day when he runs into Katie Halsey. He feels the sting of remorse, but Katie seems lively. They have lunch, and Keating discovers a dramatic change in Katie. Her spirit is dead, and she speaks only of the joys of selflessness and charity. She tells him she suffered when he married Dominique, but that she has since learned that it is futile to fight fate. Keating tells her that he truly wanted to marry her and that the worst sin he ever committed was marrying Dominique. Keating asks Katie why people think doing what you really want is easy, when it is actually the hardest thing in the world. Katie reprimands him for being so selfish and leaves.

ANALYSIS: CHAPTERS 6–10
Keating and Wynand find themselves questioning their lives, and Rand narrates their stories side by side for comparison. Despite the great differences between Keating and Wynand, they share the opportunity for salvation through Roark. Wynand saves himself; Keating does not. Keating represents the sad fate that awaits those too ignorant to understand Roark and his values. Roark consistently

rescues Keating, and only in Chapter 8 does Keating understand that Roark helps him for the sake of architecture, not out of pity or to gain the upper hand. Without wealth and success to corrupt him, Keating finally becomes honest and realizes that architecture is not just a means to power but an actual end in itself. He becomes even more self-aware upon meeting Katie again. He sees that he has ruined her life and deadened her spirit. Keating sees the hollowness of his life at this point, but Rand judges him sternly, and Keating's realization comes too late.

Wynand's awakening comes at just the right time. Keating feels too weary to act on his repentance, but Wynand throws himself into the fight against society with vigor. Since the emergence of the *Banner*, Wynand has believed that he controls the world, and when he finds that the world actually controls him, he spares no effort to fight back. Wynand succeeds where Keating fails because Wynand was secretly ready for an awakening, whereas Keating's realizations take him completely by surprise. Keating has not marshaled the tools or desire to adapt to Roark's way of living.

Interestingly, Rand never provides a personal history of her protagonist, Howard Roark. Rand details extensive personal histories for Keating, Toohey, and Wynand in the sections named after them but never explains where or how Roark grew up, even though the fourth book of the novel is named after him. We know only that he comes from a poor family, though we know nothing about his parents or upbringing. Roark's mysterious past makes his story applicable to everyone, as if Rand wants to suggest that background has nothing to do with genius or principle. It also makes Roark the perfect man. He has no history because he does not change. He is born a creator. His lack of a family makes him even more independent and free from the influence of others. Anything that is important in his past, present, or future resides in his buildings.

This last section does, however, expand our view of Roark in two important ways: we get to look inside both his heart and his head. Rand does not want Roark to be a completely isolated human, and thus, in this section, we see him love Dominique and Wynand. Roark also makes two key declarations about his beliefs in life—the first on Wynand's yacht, in Chapter 11, and the second during the Cortlandt trial, in Chapter 18—that underscore *The Fountainhead*'s message of independence and egoism.

PART IV: CHAPTERS 11–15

SUMMARY: CHAPTER 11

> *Tell man that he must live for others. . . . Not a single one of them has ever achieved it and not a single one ever will. . . . But don't you see what you accomplish? . . . He'll obey.*
>
> (See QUOTATIONS, p. 60)

When most of the work on the Cortlandt project is done, Roark agrees to go on a long yacht voyage with Wynand. As Roark and Wynand sail, they talk about the true definition of selflessness. Roark defines selfless people as "second-handers" who live their lives through others. Roark says the greatest enemy of the second-hander is an independent spirit.

SUMMARY: CHAPTER 12

When Roark returns to New York, he visits the Cortlandt construction site and finds that his plans have been altered. His substructure remains unchanged, but new features cover the building's façade. Toohey's protégées secretly made these additions. Keating fought desperately to uphold the integrity of the building, but the interlopers overwhelmed him. Roark goes to see Dominique and asks her to drive past Cortlandt Homes the following Monday. She must stop in front of Cortlandt to pretend she is out of gas and send the night watchman to a gas station over a mile away. Dominique agrees, knowing that Roark only includes her so that she will not suffer later.

Dominique follows Roark's instructions. She parks in front of the Cortlandt building and asks the night watchman to help her get gas. When he leaves, Dominique steps outside and sees the Cortlandt building explode in a brilliant ball of fire. Dominique returns to her car, part of which has been crushed under a piece of machinery. She crawls into the front seat and tries to make it look like she never left the car by slashing her neck, legs, and arms with a splinter of glass. When the police arrive, Dominique is unconscious and nearly dead.

SUMMARY: CHAPTER 13

Dominique wakes up in Wynand's penthouse, where Wynand scolds her, even though he approves of destroying the building. Wynand has not yet guessed the nature of Dominique's relationship with Roark, and she feels sad when she thinks of the pain this will cause Wynand. Roark has been arrested for destroying the building. After Wynand pays Roark's bail, Roark comes to visit Dominique. Roark says if he is convicted, he wants Dominique to stay with Wynand, but if he is acquitted, he wants her to leave Wynand for him. The public denounces Roark as the enemy of the poor. Some people speculate that Roark was bitter because Keating and Webb borrowed his ideas. Wynand orders all of his papers to defend Roark, but the support of the Wynand press hurts Roark more than it helps him. Wynand begins to realize how thoroughly Toohey has corrupted his organization.

SUMMARY: CHAPTER 14
Toohey goes to see Keating, who is hiding from the media. Toohey asks Keating to admit that Roark designed the Cortlandt home because he thinks this fact will hurt Roark. Keating has become so dependent on Toohey that he cannot bear to think about Toohey's true nature, but Toohey forces Keating to understand his evil, explaining that he gains power over men by forcing them to join the cult of selflessness. Toohey's speech devastates Keating. He begs Toohey not to leave him alone. Toohey laughs.

SUMMARY: CHAPTER 15
Toohey publishes a column criticizing Roark, and Wynand has Toohey and the editors who approved the column fired. Toohey promises Wynand that when he returns, he will own the paper. The Union of Wynand Employees, which is made up of dedicated Toohey followers, goes on strike to demand the reinstatement of Toohey and the other editors. They also demand a complete reversal of the paper's pro-Roark policy. Wynand runs the paper with a skeleton crew. The picket lines outside become violent, and a few of the remaining employees are injured when they enter the building in the morning. Wynand works fiercely and Dominique moves into the *Banner* building to help him in any way she can. Every day, however, they print fewer copies of the *Banner,* and even those copies go unsold.

ANALYSIS: CHAPTERS 11–15
Roark's bombing of the Cortlandt building is the novel's climax, as the opposing forces in the novel come into all-out conflict. The bombing marks the first gesture of defiance by the talented few against the mediocre majority. Although Roark is the one who actu-

ally bombs the building, all of the major figures are involved: Keating officially designs the building, Toohey corrupts it, and Dominique aids and watches Roark's destruction of it. Roark never before reacts to Toohey's provocations, but never before does Toohey physically alter Roark's work. When Roark reacts, he does so in characteristic fashion, taking firm, irrevocable action that leaves no room for counter-arguments. A less ideal man might have filed a lawsuit or even, like Stephen Mallory, made a futile attempt to kill Toohey, but Roark takes final action to destroy the blasphemy against his design.

Roark reacts differently to the Cortlandt building than to the Stoddard Temple because the temple is completed according to his specifications and altered later. He does not care what the world does with his finished buildings but insists on finishing his buildings as he wishes. The Cortlandt complex perverts Roark's ideas before they have been implemented. Unable to tolerate this kind of compromise, Roark must destroy the mediocrity to maintain his integrity.

The bombing seals Dominique and Roark's love. Dominique has been unable to abandon the world completely and has been torn between society and Roark. Now she signals her renewed allegiance to Roark by helping him bomb the building. Dominique has always been stimulated by violence, and the bombing sets her free and makes her ready to resume her relationship with Roark. Her lifelessness following the explosion is part of her rebirth; with the annihilation of the Cortlandt comes the annihilation of her resistance to the world. We later learn that when Dominique cuts herself in the car, it is her final act of masochism. The violent destruction of the Cortlandt building heals Dominique and reconciles her with the man she loves.

In the chapters before and after the novel's climax, Rand sums up the ideology of the novel by giving both Roark and Toohey two lengthy philosophical monologues. These two monologues serve the same role as closing arguments in a courtroom, a last chance for each side to make its point. Rand employs setting and tone to indicate that we should prefer Roark's monologue. Roark, the novel's idol and savior, discusses his beliefs on the importance of the ego in the serene setting of a luxury yacht trip. He speaks to Wynand, his close friend, and his speech is calm, amicable, and reassuring. Toohey goes on his tirade in Keating's claustrophobic, shabby apartment. He expresses his philosophy of selflessness as he terrorizes the pathetic, beaten-down Keating. By giving Roark's monologue such a serene tone and Toohey's such a fearful one, Rand does not so much ask us to choose a side as remind us that Roark's has always been the correct one.

PART IV: CHAPTERS 16–20

SUMMARY: CHAPTER 16

The board of investors of the *Banner* calls an emergency meeting. Many of the paper's advertisers have left and the paper is inching toward ruin. Wynand knows he will have to shut down the *Banner* if he does not compromise. He walks the streets of New York in torment. In the end, Wynand gives in. As he does so, he has the distinct sensation of putting a gun to his head and pulling the trigger. The next day, the *Banner* prints a formal apology for defending Roark, signed by Wynand.

SUMMARY: CHAPTER 17

People all over the city see the headline and buy the paper. Roark forgives Wynand in a letter, but Wynand returns the letter unopened. Dominique goes to Roark's house in Monadnock Valley. Roark almost rejects her for Wynand's sake, but realizes that she is right in thinking that Wynand will never recover his lost principles. Dominique finally feels complete enough to love Roark forever and they make love to consummate their renewed relationship. The next morning, Dominique calls the local police to report a stolen ring. The police arrive with two reporters, and when Dominique greets them in Roark's pajamas, she makes it obvious that she and Roark are sleeping together. Dominique explains to Roark that she wants the scandal to unite them against the world.

The story about Dominique and Roark appears in every newspaper in New York. Alvah Scarret advises Wynand to divorce Dominique and Wynand agrees. When Wynand returns home, he finds Dominique waiting. She tells him that Roark is the man she has always loved. Later, Guy Francon calls. Dominique expects him to be angry, but he is glad because he knows Roark is the right man for her. Scarret wants to use the Dominique scandal to bolster the paper's poor circulation. Wynand agrees, and the *Banner* runs an article saying that Dominique forced Wynand to defend her lover. Thousands of letters of condolence pour in and the public forgives Wynand.

SUMMARY: CHAPTER 18

Roark represents himself at his trial. He deliberately chooses the least sympathetic jury possible. When Keating is called to the witness stand, he lifelessly states that Roark designed Cortlandt and that he began to fear Roark after the project changed. Roark does not call any witnesses. He declares his principles in a moving speech, describing creators as great men who feed the world with their genius. They do this because it is man's nature to seek truth and to create, not to serve their fellow man. Roark condemns "second-handers," men who feed on the souls of creators. He warns that altruism has even corrupted the great nation of the United States, a country built by brilliant men. Roark says he gave the Cortlandt to his fellow men, but he destroyed it because he could not stand to see it corrupted. The jury leaves the room briefly and then finds Roark not guilty. Roark looks at Wynand, who leaves without a word.

Summary: Chapter 19

The millionaire Roger Enright purchases the Cortlandt site from the government and hires Roark to rebuild the project. The new housing complex will charge reasonable rents for tenants of all incomes while still making a profit for Enright. The city's labor board orders Wynand to rehire Toohey. Toohey returns to his office and tries to ignore Wynand. After ten minutes, the presses stop and Wynand informs Toohey that the *Banner* no longer exists and that Toohey is out of a job. Toohey goes to work for an upscale New York paper and immediately begins making inquiries about the publisher's beliefs. A few months later, Roark visits Wynand in Wynand's office. Wynand asks Roark to design a structure to be called the Wynand Building as an act of defiance against the world. Wynand tells Roark to design the building as a monument to the spirit that Roark possesses.

Summary: Chapter 20

Eighteen months later, Dominique walks to the construction site of the Wynand Building. She steps onto an outside hoist that lifts her up past the finished masonry line and into the naked steel and space of the building. At the very top of the building, so high that he is the only thing visible besides the ocean and the sky, stands her husband, Howard Roark.

Analysis: Chapters 16–20

When Wynand must choose between his paper and his principles, he finds himself in a situation Roark has faced many times. Roark always does the right, principled thing, and Wynand does not. Both men have to choose between closing their offices and compromising their principles, but whereas Roark chose to become a physical laborer rather than compromise, Wynand cannot bring himself to throw away his life's work. Instead, he chooses to save his paper, even though this decision robs his life of meaning. Wynand becomes a tragic figure because he does not act with weak ignorance, as does someone like Keating. He has the capacity to succeed, and fails despite it. When Wynand first sacrifices himself for the sake of power, the failure seems understandable, because his cynicism comes from deep disillusionment. Wynand finds a chance for redemption after meeting with Roark, and Wynand's fall seems all the more tragic because it happens as he stands on the verge of redemption. Wynand does not even gain fame or fortune at the expense of his self-respect, for in the end he closes the paper down rather than rehiring Toohey. Not only does Wynand commit emotional suicide, he does so for the sake of a paper he will destroy.

The novel's final images evoke the first scene in the novel. When Dominique climbs the unfinished Wynand building to see Roark, she rises up past a cityscape full of the same hard, beautiful, and natural elements that surround Roark when he stands naked over the cliffs in the first chapter. In the final chapter, Roark stands on a skyscraper he has created, as if he has seized the elements in the first chapter and made them even more beautiful with his genius. Just as Roark laughs at the beginning of the novel, scorning convention and reveling in his independence, so now, at the end of the novel, does he stand apart from the mediocrity of the world below him. The novel closes with the statement that "there was only the ocean and the sky and the figure of Howard Roark." This elevation of Roark by comparing him to such profound bodies as the ocean and sky is a virtual deification of Roark, a declaration that his spirit alone matters. The end of the novel feels triumphant because Roark has survived unchanged, not because the rest of the world has changed. Collectivism and altruism thrive, and Toohey already schemes again, planning another rise to power. The only thing that matters, however, is that these forces have not succeeded in destroying Roark. Rand's philosophy does not seek to affect the whole world. She does not want to change people's minds, but to reach and encourage the people who already think like she does. Roark does not succeed in winning over the whole world, but he does manage to defend his own ideas and inspire others, and this is the only triumph the novel requires.

Important Quotations Explained

1. When they lay in bed together it was—as it had to be . . . an act of violence. . . . it was the moment made of hatred, tension, pain.

This quotation, from the eighth chapter of the novel's second book, describes the early relationship between Dominique and Roark. Their passion feeds on force and struggle. At this point in the novel, Roark and Dominique are both lovers and antagonists—they sleep together at night and Dominique tries to destroy Roark by day. She wants to test him to see whether he is truly the principled man he seems. The novel abhors compassion and warmth, and the violence of Roark's relationship with Dominique turns the fuzziness of love into something hard and tough, and therefore, for Rand, admirable. This quotation evokes the violence of their first sexual encounter, a highly idealized rape that Rand endorses for its cold brutality. Rand contrasts this love between two strong personalities with the whiny and comfortable love between Katie and Keating. Katie and Keating's cuddling leads to painful codependence, but the tough, combative love of Dominique and Roark produces power and free thought.

2. [Y]ou've gone beyond the probable and made us see
the possible, but possible only through you. Because
your figures are more devoid of contempt of humanity
than any work I've ever seen. . . . I came for a simple,
selfish reason . . . to seek the best.

Roark gives Stephen Mallory this pep talk in the eleventh chapter of
the novel's second book. Here Roark shows that when evaluating
people, he considers only ability and honesty. Personality and status
mean nothing to Roark, who only connects with "the best"—people who do original and inspiring work. The visit is "selfish," for
despite Roark's perfection, he feels enriched by his connections with
good people. The first half of this quotation sums up Roark's ethos.
He calls the achievements of artists like himself and Mallory the
"possible," a hopeful contrast to the boring, plodding, "probable"
everyday world. But he stresses that these achievements can come
"only through you"—that is, only through the individual artist.
Roark feels that worthwhile art must come from the artist alone,
with no input from society.

QUOTATIONS

3.   He was not the corrupt publisher of a popular empire. He was an aristocrat aboard a yacht. He looked, she thought, like what one believes an aristocrat to be when one is young: a brilliant kind of gaiety without guilt.

Rand uses physical characteristics to illustrate her characters' personalities. This quotation from the ninth chapter of the third book of *The Fountainhead* shows a physical symbol of Wynand's redemption. Dominique looks at Wynand sitting on his yacht and muses that his gestures and carriage reveal his true self. She thought him an evil publisher at first, but now sees that he has become an idealized aristocrat. Like Roark, Wynand is tall and carries himself with confidence. He moves quickly, showing his vibrancy. He is on a yacht, surrounded by luxury that would overwhelm most people, but his "brilliant kind of gaiety" overwhelms his surroundings. The once-suicidal Wynand has changed his worldview, becoming optimistic, and his new personality is so forceful that it overwhelms the facts. Technically he is still a "corrupt publisher," but his good intentions so overwhelm that technicality that the quotation says Wynand "was not the corrupt publisher."

4. Howard, I'm a parasite. I've been a parasite all my
life . . . I have fed on you and all the men like you who
lived before we were born. . . . if they hadn't existed I
wouldn't have known how to put stone to stone. . . . I
have taken that which was not mine and given
nothing in return.

Peter Keating admits his failing to Howard Roark in Chapter 8 of
the novel's final book. Roark calls men like Keating "second-handers" because they do not create original work, but steal the work of
others. After years of chasing fame and money, Keating finally looks
inside his soul and sees the pointlessness of his existence. Too late,
Keating tries to save himself by admitting his failure and humbly
asking Roark for help. The passage employs ruthless images to
show the fallacy of Keating's life. Keating describes himself as a
"parasite," something less than human. He fed on Roark point-
lessly, failing to acquire his life force. Keating is exhausted now,
while Roark thrives. Keating bares his soul in this monologue as
Roark and Toohey do in their own monologues. Together, the three
men voice Rand's worldview.

5.   Tell man that he must live for others. . . . Not a single
     one of them has ever achieved it and not a single one
     ever will. His every living impulse screams against it.
     But don't you see what you accomplish? . . . He'll obey.
     . . . Use big vague words. 'Universal Harmony'—
     'Eternal Spirit'— 'Divine Purpose'—'Nirvana'—
     'Paradise'—'Racial Supremacy'—'The Dictatorship of
     the Proletariat.'

Toohey makes this speech to a terrified Keating in the fourteenth
chapter of the last book of *The Fountainhead*. Here Toohey reveals
his true nature for the first and only time. Everything else he says is
purposefully empty of real meaning, so only here do we see the sinis-
ter inner workings of Toohey's mind. When Toohey defines "big
vague words," he uses concepts from real-world ideologies and reli-
gions. The moment is an unusual one in the novel, for usually Rand
writes about a hypothetical, imagined New York, using allegory to
reveal the flaws she sees in society. In this passage, however, she steps
from the allegorical world into the real world, telling us exactly
which groups she abhors, and exactly which groups she means to pil-
lory with her allegory. Rand wants us to condemn every concept the
arch-villain Toohey support. He uses the religious phrases "Eternal
Spirit," "Divine Purpose," "Paradise," "Nirvana," and "Universal
Harmony," suggesting Rand's low opinion of organized religion like
Christianity and Buddhism. "Racial Supremacy" and "The Dictator-
ship of the Proletariat" refer to and condemn, respectively, Nazism
and Communism. Rand thought almost all kinds of social engineering restricted individual liberty, and makes this point in the novel by
having her arch-villain refer to these catchphrases as his tools.

KEY FACTS

FULL TITLE
  The Fountainhead

AUTHOR
  Ayn Rand

TYPE OF WORK
  Novel

GENRE
  Allegory; Objectivist fiction; novel of ideas

LANGUAGE
  English

TIME AND PLACE WRITTEN
  New York, 1938–1942

DATE OF FIRST PUBLICATION
  May, 1943

PUBLISHER
  Bobbs-Merrill, New York.

NARRATOR
  The omniscient narrator provides psychological analyses of the
  characters and exhibits a heavy bias toward the novel's hero,
  Howard Roark

POINT OF VIEW
  Third person

TONE
  Formal; moralizing; didactic

TENSE
  Present, with occasional forays into past tense when explaining
  the background of some characters

SETTING (TIME)
  1922–1939

SETTING (PLACE)
New York City, Connecticut, Monadnock Valley,
Massachusets, Ohio

PROTAGONIST
Howard Roark

MAJOR CONFLICT
Howard Roark's genius and striking architectural vision
clashes with the mediocre society around him, represented by
Ellsworth Toohey

RISING ACTION
Keating succeeds financially while Roark struggles; Roark and
Dominique meet and fall in love; Roark agrees to design a
government housing complex on Keating's behalf; in Roark's
absence, Keating makes changes to get the commission

CLIMAX
Roark bombs the housing complex to prevent the corruption of
his designs

FALLING ACTION
Roark successfully defends himself at trial for the bombing;
Roark and Dominique marry

THEMES
The primacy of the individual; the importance of reason; the
cold ferocity of love

MOTIFS
Technical progress; journalism; labor

SYMBOLS
Granite; ice; the *Banner*

FORESHADOWING
When Roark finishes the Stoddard Temple, Roark must defend
himself in a lawsuit.

Study Questions & Essay Topics

Study Questions

1. *What purpose does the encounter between Roark and the Dean serve? What concepts and beliefs does the Dean represent?*

Like many of the characters in the novel, the Dean has no sense of self or integrity, and consequently cannot create his own philosophy or beliefs. When he tells Roark that everything worth building has already been done, the Dean reveals the foolishness that comes from adhering too strongly to tradition. Instead of creating innovative designs, the Dean feeds from the thoughts and beliefs of his predecessors, which he calls "treasure mines"—an image that evokes wealth and forced labor. Because of men like the Dean, everyone at the architectural school has looked only to the past for inspiration and the students have been generating the same designs for years. Roark labels this sort of weakness "second-handedness." More generally, the Dean represents how a cooperative and collectivist spirit can lead to an individual's enslavement to the desires of others. When he tells Roark to think of "the Client," the Dean shows that he believes in prioritizing the buyer over the artist, the other over the self. Whereas Roark does not assign much importance to his clients, the Dean considers them the most important voice, and in doing so surrenders his own will and initiative.

2.   *Why does the novel sanction Roark's egoism but not Toohey's? Since the novel encourages the single-minded realization of one's goals, why does Rand disapprove of Toohey's quest for domination?*

By the end of the last section it becomes clear that we are meant to read Toohey not as a leader of men, but a power-hungry villain who uses the notion of "selflessness" to break peoples' spirits. On the other hand, Toohey can be read as a model for the behavior that *The Fountainhead* advocates. Like Roark, Toohey is only interested in his own advancement. In his manipulative way, Toohey matches Roark in strength. Although he flatters people and defers to them, he only does so until he gets what he wants, and he never actually lets them get the upper hand. Roark insists on following one's principles unswervingly; in a sense, Toohey does just that. His principles involve undermining people's creative drive and becoming powerful himself, and he sticks to these principles unswervingly. Despite their similarities, however, a critical difference separates the two men: Roark creates and Toohey destroys. In *The Fountainhead*, the creation of something great justifies even the most rampant egoism. Toohey possesses rampant egoism, but no creativity. He seeks to prevent other peoples' achievements rather than to create his own achievements. Even though Toohey displays many of the virtues touted by the novel, he becomes the villain because he does not act in the name of creativity.

3.   *How does Rand justify the use of violence?*
     Specifically, how does she justify Roark's bombing of
     the Cortlandt Complex?

The Fountainhead idolizes strength, austerity, and determination
above all else, and violence progresses naturally from these virtues.
The novel frowns upon pity and compassion and advocates the use
of violence to advance human genius. Dominique embodies this
viewpoint, constantly battling the world and welcoming the occa-
sionally physical pain this battle inflicts on her. When Roark rapes
Dominique, the violence of the incident makes her come alive.
Dominique approves of Roark's destruction of the Cortlandt Complex, and helps him destroy it. Dominique considers violent acts
both passionate and assertive. Passion and assertiveness also char-
acterize genius, so violence becomes indicative of genius. Roark
does not share Dominique's great enthusiasm for violence, but he
has no qualms about using it in defense of his beliefs or ideas. Roark
considers bombing Cortlandt a necessity, an act to accomplish with
workmanlike dispassion. Overall, Rand supports Roark's view of
violence as a tool like any other: neither good nor bad, but sometimes necessary.

SUGGESTED ESSAY TOPICS

1. Does Peter Keating genuinely love Dominique Francon? Why or why not?

2. What similarities do Keating and Roark share? Why does Rand make them somewhat similar?

3. Why does Gail Wynand take so much comfort in the knowledge that both he and Roark "came from nothing"?

4. Dominique admits that she and Wynand are very similar people. How is this true? How are they different?

5. *The Fountainhead* was written during the rise of totalitarian states in Europe and Russia. How might the events of this period have affected Rand's novel?

6. How does *The Fountainhead* portray women? How do Dominique and Catherine measure up to the male characters?

REVIEW & RESOURCES

QUIZ

1. Where does Howard Roark stay during his years at Stanton?

   A. A small housing project
   B. The Keating family's home
   C. The shabbiest dorm building
   D. With his engineering professor

2. Why does Peter Keating choose to go to New York and work for Guy Francon?

   A. Roark suggests he do so
   B. Peter secretly hopes to begin an art career there
   C. Peter's mother manipulates him into moving
   D. Peter has heard that Guy Francon's daughter is very beautiful

3. Why does Henry Cameron initially ask Roark to leave his office?

   A. Cameron does not want Roark to suffer at the hands of the world
   B. Roark does not accept anyone else's authority
   C. Cameron's firm is bankrupt and he cannot afford Roark
   D. Cameron's richest client despises Roark

4. What is Roark's first building?

   A. The Stoddard Temple
   B. The Heller House
   C. The Cosmo-Slotnick Building
   D. The Enright House

5. Why does Roark go work in Connecticut?

    A. He cannot afford to keep his New York office open
    B. He knows that Dominique is spending the summer there
    C. He feels he needs more experience in a workman's trade to complete his education
    D. Wynand has ensured that no one in the city will hire him

6. Why does Roark send another worker in his place to set the marble stone in Dominique's fireplace?

    A. He knows that if she sees him again, she will fire him
    B. His friend needs the money more than Roark does
    C. He has received a letter from Roger Enright calling him to New York
    D. He wants to show Dominique that she needs him

7. Why does Dominique criticize the drawings of the Enright House?

    A. She feels the world does not deserve such perfection
    B. She knows it is technically unsound
    C. She thinks it does not have enough character
    D. She is a great admirer of Peter Keating and wishes to help him

8. Why is Gail Wynand's yacht called *I Do*?

    A. It is Wynand's response to every man who ever told him, "You don't run things around here"
    B. It is an ironic reference to his notorious bachelor life
    C. It is a declaration of Wynand's affinity with the public will
    D. It is a response to Dominique's marriage proposal

9. Why does Roark accept the Stoddard commission even though he has serious reservations about it?

  A. Stoddard impresses him
  B. Roark does not want Peter Keating to botch such an incredible project
  C. Toohey has coached Stoddard to say precisely what Roark needs to hear
  D. Roark is nearly bankrupt and needs the commission very badly

10. Why does Stephen Mallory try to kill Ellsworth Toohey?

  A. Because Toohey used his influence to rob Mallory of a commission
  B. Because Mallory understands that Toohey represents a dangerous and malicious kind of cunning
  C. Because Mallory does not want Toohey to interfere with Roark's career
  D. Because Mallory wishes to go to prison

11. On whose behalf does Dominique craftily testify at the Stoddard Trial?

  A. On Stoddard's behalf
  B. On Toohey's behalf
  C. On Mallory's behalf
  D. She does not testify

12. What is the first thing we see Gail Wynand doing?

  A. Sailing his yacht
  B. Writing a letter to the President
  C. Walking through New York
  D. Holding a gun to his temple

REVIEW & RESOURCES

13. Why does Toohey send Wynand the statue of Dominique?

   A. To atone for an earlier offense
   B. To convince Wynand to destroy the model and
      the sculptor
   C. To rouse Wynand's interest in Dominique
   D. To improve his public image by adding to Wynand's
      famous gallery

14. Why does Mike love Roark?

   A. Because Roark gave him his first electrician's job
   B. Because Mike admires skill in every form, and Roark
      is supremely gifted
   C. Because Mike loves all architects
   D. Because Roark stays far away from building sites,
      giving Mike more freedom to work

15. Why does Dominique suddenly regret her marriage to
   Gail Wynand and feel sorry for him?

   A. Wynand is nobler than she expected, and she knows
      that she does not truly love him
   B. She thinks that Roark will punish Wynand
   C. Wynand is a worse scoundrel than she thought, and
      she feels surprised by him
   D. She feels that he is too subservient to his staff

16. Why is Roark hired to design the Monadnock Valley resort?

   A. Because his brilliant design will mean the homes can
      be rented at an incredible profit
   B. Because the governing board believes he is the worst
      architect in the country
   C. Because Toohey suggests him to the board, knowing that
      the entire project will soon collapse in yet another scandal
   D. Because Austen Heller fights on his behalf

17. How does Roark defend himself at the Stoddard trial?

   A. He submits only photographs of the temple
   B. He agrees to pay the fine but begs the judge to let the building stand as it is
   C. He reads a brief, stunning statement
   D. He appears heavily intoxicated and stands silent

18. How does Dominique change Gail Wynand?

   A. She forces him to face the truth about the society that his paper serves
   B. She teaches him to write architecture columns
   C. She buys him a yacht
   D. She is the first woman he sleeps with

19. What is the Council of American Builders?

   A. An electrician's union of which Mike is a member
   B. An advocacy group that works on Roark's behalf
   C. A council of young architects handpicked by Toohey
   D. A radical terrorist group responsible for bombing the Cortlandt complex

20. What does Dominique do after Roark destroys the Cortlandt Homes?

   A. She flees to Cameron's house in New Jersey
   B. She blames Wynand for the crime
   C. She slashes herself with glass and passes out in her car
   D. She agrees to pay for its reconstruction

21. For the Cortlandt trial, what kind of men does Roark look for when selecting the jury?

   A. Jurors who seem compassionate
   B. Jurors who are demolition experts
   C. A select group of friends and colleagues
   D. The least sympathetic group possible

22. At whom does Roark first look after he is acquitted?

    A. Dominique
    B. Wynand
    C. Mike
    D. Toohey

23. How does Dominique make her affair with Roark public?

    A. She writes and publishes an article in the *Banner*
    B. She calls the police from his home to report a missing ring
    C. She holds a press conference in the Cord Building
    D. She gets a private detective to take pictures of her with Roark and then sends them to Toohey

24. Why does Wynand hire Roark to design the Wynand Building?

    A. He wants Roark to make the statement he himself could never make
    B. He wants to redeem himself
    C. He wants to win back Dominique
    D. He feels his old building is too cramped

25. What does Roark do after Wynand and the *Banner* abandon him?

    A. He publicly denounces Wynand
    B. He forgives Wynand in a letter
    C. He blows up the *Banner*'s offices
    D. He goes to a church to pray

Suggestions for Further Reading

DEN UYL, DOUGLAS J. THE FOUNTAINHEAD: *An American Novel.*
New York: Twayne Publishers, 1999.

GLADSTEIN, MIMI REISEL. *The New Ayn Rand Companion.*
Westport, Connecticut: Greenwood Press, 1999.

———— AND CHRIS SCIABARRA, EDS. *Feminist Interpretations of
Ayn Rand.* University Park: Pennsylvania State University
Press, 1999.

KELLEY, DAVID. *The Contested Legacy of Ayn Rand: Truth and
Toleration in Objectivism.* Poughkeepsie, New York:
Objectivist Center; New Brunswick, New Jersey: Transaction
Publishers, 2000.

RAND, AYN. *The Romantic Manifesto; a Philosophy of Literature.*
New York: World Publishing Company, 1969.

————. *Atlas Shrugged.* New York: Random House, 1957.

————, NATHANIEL BRANDON, ALAN GREENSPAN, AND ROBERT
HESSEN. *Capitalism: The Unknown Ideal.* New York: New
American Library, 1966.

SCIABARRA, CHRIS MATTHEW. *Ayn Rand: The Russian Radical.*
University Park: Pennsylvania State University Press, 1995.

WALKER, JEFF. *Ayn Rand Cult.* Chicago: Open Court, 1999.

SparkNotes Study Guides: